Praise for *Will Work for Fun*

"Fun, fun, and more fun. Alan R. Bechtold has written the best step-by-step formula for moving your work and your life from boring to exhilarating that I've ever read. Work truly can be play and Alan R. Bechtold shows you how."
> —Kris Solie-Johnson, Chancellor, American Institute of Small Business, http://www.aisb.biz/

"In *Will Work for Fun*, Alan Bechtold gives us a glimpse of a lifestyle we all dream of, yet have not found possible. The book is fun, and the systems Alan teaches can help you live the life you always dreamed of."
> —Warren Whitlock, Book Marketing Strategist, BestSellerAuthors.com

"Alan R. Bechtold unlocks the vault so you can have fun . . . make money . . . and enjoy the lifestyle of your dreams. This isn't just a book. This is a roadmap to success and happiness. Now you can have both!"
> —Michael Penland, http://www.instantcashmarketing.com

Will Work for Fun

Three Simple Steps for Turning Any Hobby or Interest into Cash

Alan R. Bechtold

WILEY

John Wiley & Sons, Inc.

Published by John Wiley & Sons, Inc., Hoboken, New Jersey.

Published simultaneously in Canada.

For general information on our other products and services or for technical support, please contact our Customer Care Department within the United States at (800) 762-2974, outside the United States at (317) 572-3993 or fax (317) 572-4002.

Wiley also publishes its books in a variety of electronic formats. Some content that appears in print may not be available in electronic books. For more information about Wiley products, visit our web site at www.wiley.com.

Library of Congress Cataloging-in-Publication Data

Bechtold, Alan R., 1952-
  Will work for fun : three simple steps for turning any hobby or interest into cash / Alan R. Bechtold.
      p.   cm.
  Includes bibliographical references and index.
  ISBN 978-0-470-23179-1 (cloth)
  1.   Self-employed. 2.   Quality of work life. 3.   Electronic commerce–Management. 4.   Internet marketing. 5.   Internet publishing. I. Title.
  HD8036.B43 2008
  658'.041–dc22

                                                                    2007043559

Printed in the United States of America

10 9 8 7 6 5 4 3 2 1

CONTENTS

Contents

ACKNOWLEDGMENTS

To Carol: Without you, I could never have written this book—or lived through what I've lived through to be able to write this book. Putting up with me all day every day would be enough for most, but you also put up with me through the three-month process I went through writing this book, on top of my already-busy schedule. You make every moment of my life even better.

To Mark Joyner: for hooking me up with the great folks at John Wiley and Sons. You have for many years been my spark of inspiration, but you were also the spark that made this book happen. I will be forever grateful. It's *sympathy poker* time!

To Dr. Joe Vitale: I am always amazed at the life you're living. I've found much to admire in you, and I'm certain you will continue to exceed even your dreams.

To my family, friends, partners, and associates: My life has been wonderful. You are all an integral reason why. May your every day be as blessed as mine.

To Mom: You've always been there for me and believed in me.

And especially, to my brother, Stan: Sorry if I picked on you a little in the book. You've had plenty of reasons to be totally frustrated with me, but you love me anyway. You'll never know how much that means to me.

FOREWORD

Alan is one of my favorite Internet marketers. He's funny, friendly, prolific, and profitable.

He may be the only person on earth who has been successfully and profitably publishing and marketing online for more than 23 years. During that time, he's averaged more than $1 million in sales per year doing what he loves most:

- When Alan was studying to write science fiction, he started a newsletter and support group for science fiction writers. As a result, he was able to work directly with some of the biggest names in science fiction, including Arthur C. Clarke, Ray Bradbury, and Isaac Asimov.

- Alan fell in love with video games, so he launched a newspaper reviewing new video games and received hundreds of free games and complete video game systems—and made money playing with them.

- When Alan discovered computers, he launched a syndicated electronic news column about computers and software. He received thousands of dollars' worth of free software and generated a solid profit.

- When music CDs were first introduced, Alan started an electronic publication that reviewed them and syndicated the column through the online network of computer bulletin board systems he'd built. He received literally thousands of free music CDs and made money from subscription fees.

- When the World Wide Web exploded, Alan's publishing experience enabled him to quickly jump to the Web, where he has since generated millions of dollars doing what he loves doing most—publishing and marketing on the Web.

- On the Web, Alan currently publishes three weekly electronic newsletters with a combined readership of more than 45,000. He also conducts a minimum of one teleseminar per week. More than 6,500 people registered for his most recent teleseminar. He also publishes a printed monthly newsletter that is mailed to more than 300 subscribers who pay $97 per month to receive it.

It should come as no surprise to you that his book is packed with information, stories, inspiration, and more. Alan has been around the block when it comes to having fun while making money. Now he's opened his brain and let you peek inside to his inner workings.

I think this book is a masterpiece of how-to information for the newbie as well as the seasoned pro. Heck, I learned a lot reading it, too. But more than anything else, you'll read this and discover how to make the work you do for a living FUN!

Read and grow rich.

—Dr. Joe Vitale
www.mrfire.com

PROLOGUE: "WHY DON'T THEY *STOP*?"

The true object of all human life is play. Earth is a task garden; heaven is a playground.

—G. K. Chesterton

If you could find a way to make more money doing what you love doing most, to add to what you make at your present job or, possibly, to even eventually *replace* that income altogether—wouldn't that be a far better way to live? Wouldn't that make you feel differently about the very nature of the work that you do? Isn't it possible that this would create a situation where you would find that you enjoy every moment that you're working so much that you'd have a hard time stopping?

Just ask Paul McCartney.

I've been a Beatles fan all my life. I finally got my first chance to see Paul McCartney perform live, with his band, Wings, in Kansas City. It was several years ago, during Paul's first solo tour after he decided to perform songs he originally performed with the Beatles. It was a *killer* show!

I couldn't help looking around Arrowhead Stadium, noticing it was filled to the brim with thousands of people. There wasn't a single empty seat anywhere. This started me thinking about all the money this one show was generating for my favorite Beatle. Then I added up the number of similar performances he's given since the breakup of one of my favorite rock bands of all time.

Most of us could live comfortably the rest of our lives on the revenues generated during this one Kansas City show. Paul's tour that year included 13 *other shows*! And he's been actively writing, recording, and touring, virtually nonstop, since the Beatles broke up.

Wow!

Then I wondered—why was Paul on the road at all? I was glad that he was. If he never toured again after the Beatles, I'd never have had that chance to see him perform live. But, in spite of the fact that he flew to each show in a private jet, from an island base in the Bahamas ... in spite of the fact that road crews set everything up before he stepped out to play ... the road is never easy—and Paul isn't a kid any more.

But, here was Paul, hitting the stage in Kansas City and other places around the world, working long hours, flying back and forth, from city to city.

It's not that Paul needs the money. He's been ranked as England's wealthiest musician, with a net worth of roughly $750 million.

While I watched Paul play, I saw the *real* reason why he was still onstage, touring and playing live, long after he could have simply retired and spent his days relaxing, traveling, and enjoying a retirement you and I can only dream about having. It was written all over his face.

Paul was having a *blast* belting out those songs, playing to the crowd and feeling their joy. I'm reasonably certain, from what I saw, that fun is squarely behind the song writing, recording, and performing Paul still does to this day.

You might think it unfair of me to bring up Paul McCartney as an illustration of the FUN Money lifestyle I'm going to show you how to achieve in this book. But, believe it or not, you can live a rock-star lifestyle whether you play an instrument, with or without writing talent, with or without any talent of any kind—when you follow the simple formula I'll deliver to you shortly.

A MILLION TO ONE

Remember—for every Paul McCartney who makes it and actually lands even one hit record, there are *thousands* of performers who still go onstage night after night, touring in buses, hauling their own equipment and setting it up themselves, usually for little or no money, often working day jobs just to pay the bills and eat. And they persist precisely because it's so much *fun* . . . and there is always the chance, however slight, that one day they *might* be able to do it for a living.

That's one of the *tests* you can apply to determine whether you've discovered a good source of FUN Money for you. If you love doing something so much you now *pay* to do it, and you work another job just to support yourself so you can *keep* doing it every chance you get (which is probably all too rare)—that thing could be a perfect source of FUN Money for you!

Almost anything you truly love doing can be turned into money using my simple formula. The trick is the way you approach turning what you do into money. The arts, for example, are notorious FUN Money sources. Writing, painting, photography, acting, and music certainly qualify because they are all things we imagine would be fun to do for a living.

Unfortunately, most artists aren't marketers. They don't necessarily know how to *sell* what they create, so they keep working part-time, or they pursue their art part-time and work full-time, just to eat and keep producing, hoping for the day they're discovered and get their big break.

Sadly, this rarely leads to success.

Apply my three simple FUN Money formula steps, however, and you can turn your artistic endeavors into an endless source of joy by making them pay for your fun—with a profit—*while* you play.

Even better, the arts aren't your only choice. This is a good thing, since most of us aren't especially artistic, and we don't particularly think painting or writing or playing a musical instrument is the most fun thing we can do with the neighbors watching.

I don't think anyone would consider Donald Trump a player in the arts. Yet, he's the perfect example of someone who could have thrown in the towel *years* ago, to live on a deserted island (or anywhere else he wants to live) and spend the rest of his days on earth like royalty.

Instead, "The Donald" continues working bigger and bigger deals, amassing more millions and billions of dollars in the process. Even when he got into financial trouble and faced complete collapse and bankruptcy in the early 1990s, he kept pushing forward and eventually, after nearly a decade, returned to the rosy financial situation he now enjoys, with a net worth of somewhere close to $3 *billion.*

And, still he keeps working like a madman, hours on end, day in and day out.

He explained his motivation: Donald Trump lives for the next *big* deal. He loves every minute of putting huge deals together and seeing them through to completion. Real estate development is just one of the main vehicles for the deals he likes to put together.

The point, once again, is that he's still doing it, and he continues long after he needs the money, because he *loves* what he's doing.

WHAT WOULD *YOU* DO?

If we had the kind of money Trump or McCartney has, most of us would simply retire. Under the "old" philosophy about work, anyone who keeps doing what they did to make those millions or billions is a workaholic. Right? Not necessarily!

Bill Gates is another example. He never has to work ever again and hasn't had to for more than a decade. Yet, he's still at Microsoft, still involved in the development of new software and hardware products, still working in the company he founded. Gates could easily quit tomorrow. But, he loves technology, computers, and business-building too much to stop.

I probably don't have to provide much explanation for why Hugh Hefner keeps doing what he does. Or why he loves doing it.

Compare these examples to your life and what you do to earn a living. If you were handed one million dollars in cash—what would you do?

I'll bet you would at least think about quitting your job! You're not alone.

According to the first-ever survey of National Lottery winners (conducted recently by Camelot Group PLC, operator of the U.K. National Lottery), 56 percent of winners of more than £ 1 million have given up working.

You can't really blame them, can you? Most jobs suck. Most people who play the lottery do so dreaming that, one day, they'll hit it big. And, if that unlikely day arrives, then—finally!—they can quit work to start *enjoying* life.

Ask yourself—have you ever heard of many big lottery winners who say they're looking forward to continuing with their jobs? Generally speaking, it's tough for most people to imagine a job that's so much fun they'd keep doing it, even if they didn't need the money any more.

Doing work that is so much fun you'd rather work than play is simply not what we imagine our lives to hold for us—so we find a good-paying job, buckle down to work, put in our time, and pray for some relief in the form of an occasional vacation—and retirement, if we're not lucky enough to win the lottery but wind up being lucky enough to actually have a retirement waiting for us at the end of our careers.

We've all heard many of those horror stories about lottery winners, who wind up losing everything to greed and waste, then head back to the workforce, struggling day to day to make a living again, within just a few years of winning.

Their work didn't create the wealth they had just fall into their laps, and they don't love their work enough to understand that money is not about happiness, anyway. It's about *freedom* and *choice*.

WE CAN ALL BE ROCK STARS

The truth is you don't have to be a rock star to live like one. You don't have to win the lottery to start enjoying more of what you enjoy doing most right now. You don't have to be Bill Gates or Donald Trump or Hugh Hefner, either. All you have to do is change your attitude about the nature of work—then change what you already enjoy doing for fun into an activity that also earns you money.

From there, life gets *really* good!

However, it's not just a matter of doing what you love. The money won't somehow magically materialize just because you're doing something you love. If this were how things really worked, there'd be no such thing as a starving artist. Last time I looked, I don't think we had a shortage of out-of-work musicians and writers in the world today.

Instead, you have to follow a system. You must apply certain simple principles and start a business that involves what it is you love doing most. There is some work involved. But, it's all very easy work. When you're working on a business involving what you love doing most, the work is actually *fun*.

Follow my simple system, and you'll enjoy every minute of the process.

INTRODUCTION: THE TRUE NATURE OF WORK

People rarely succeed unless they have fun in what they are doing.

—Dale Carnegie

More than 12 years ago, I was in my basement office working on a deadline, when the phone rang. It was my brother.

I love my brother dearly and look up to him in ways he might never realize. That's why, no matter how busy I am or how tight the deadline might be, I always try to pick up the phone when he calls.

"Hey, bro. What are you doing?" he would always ask.

"I'm working on a deadline—what are you up to?" I would always reply.

"*Another* deadline?" he would then, without fail, reply. "Man! You're *always* on one deadline or another. Don't you *ever* take a break?"

He was dead-on with that zinger. It made me cringe every time I heard it because I knew where he was going with this line of questioning. I *am* always on one deadline or an other, most of the time. It seems that's my life story. But, I almost *never* get anything done that doesn't come attached to a deadline. I suppose that's why I've always published newsletters, magazines, and newspapers. They all come with deadlines that *force* me to get the work done.

It's not that I wouldn't rather go out and enjoy some time with my brother. He's one of my favorite people in the world. But, soon, I'd find myself spending all my time out doing something else if there were no deadlines attached to what I do.

At the time my brother called, I was still living in Topeka, Kansas, where I was born and raised. My wife at the time was a nurse who could earn *real* money in the outside world while I was basically a totally unemployable hopeful writer and publisher.

Finances at the time dictated that it was best that I stay home with our two children and raise them while mom worked. This allowed me to work on my writing and publishing projects on the side, in what spare time was afforded me after the children laid down for naps, went off to school, or went to bed for the night.

It was a perfect arrangement for a budding author/entrepreneur. I helped save our family hundreds of dollars per month in childcare expenses while my wife brought in a professional's salary to cover our bills.

But this schedule didn't leave much free time for hanging out with my brother, and I don't think he ever fully understood. I hope he reads this and finally understands.

"So," my ever-hopeful brother would say. "I was thinking about getting out of the house for a while. Could you get away for an hour? Maybe we could go grab a beer or catch a movie."

As always, I would sigh and say, "I'm sorry, man. I *have* to finish this newsletter before tomorrow morning and I just got the kids to bed. I don't see how I can take any time away right now. Maybe later?"

"Alan," he would say, "you're *always* working. All you do is work. Whenever I call, you don't ever have time to get away because you're always on a deadline, always working. You're a damned *workaholic!*"

This dour proclamation always made me feel like I'd just had a Phillips screwdriver pushed into my chest—slowly. Primarily because what he said was true—at least on the surface. I've always worked 10- to 12-hour days, six and sometimes seven days a week. I still work a schedule that comes pretty close to that today.

ROUND-THE-CLOCK NON-WORKAHOLIC

Still—I absolutely do *not* consider myself a workaholic.

If you find this statement confusing, given my schedule, don't feel bad. You're far from alone. The vast majority of people have the wrong idea about work. Odds are, you do, too.

Like my brother, most people were raised to believe you have to work *hard* to make a living. Most of us translate this to mean that the work we do has to be hard. Or boring. Or both. As a consequence, we've also come to believe that work isn't supposed to be fun. It's something everyone has to do to live. If you're extremely lucky, most people also believe, there might be some free time left at the end of the day, or on a weekend, or once a year—maybe during vacation—when we can do what we really *enjoy* doing—*if* there's also enough money left over after paying bills to do it.

Short of that—there's always retirement, isn't there? *If* there's enough money left over at the end of our working lives to actually retire one day; if we live long enough to get there.

The well-meaning people who taught us this had no idea that it was no longer true. Until just barely 12 years ago, it *was* true. Back when my brother would call, it was hard for anyone to imagine someone working round-the-clock and enjoying every minute of it the way I do.

But—I *do* enjoy every minute of the work I do. I enjoy it so much that it *feels* like I'm playing. My work is writing and publishing. I personally couldn't imagine anything else that I could do to have more fun.

I love watching movies and the occasional beer, too. I love my family and friends and spend time with them whenever I can. But, I'm truly happiest when I'm writing and publishing.

WORK: A DIFFERENT VIEW

Chances are, you feel the way my brother does. It might be difficult for you to understand, but my job isn't something I just do for the money. I've held regular jobs—years ago. When I did, I'd watch the clock like a hawk, counting the hours and minutes until I could clock out and race home, so I could do what I *really* enjoyed doing most—writing and publishing.

I don't work all the hours I do because I love to work. I work all those hours because I love the work I do so much it doesn't *feel* like work.

A workaholic, by my own definition, is someone who works round-the-clock at something he doesn't enjoy doing, *only* for the money. Or—it describes people for whom money is the be-all and end-all of existence. These people work round-the-clock, *killing* themselves to get their hands on as much cash as they can, as if, somehow, someone else will manage to grab it all if they don't get it first.

That most certainly doesn't describe me or what I do for a living.

What would you call someone who plays tennis professionally? They love the game. They work hard at it constantly, for hours on end every day. They're on the road all the time, playing in tournaments or recording endorsement commercials, often working seven days a week, 10 or 12 hours a day.

If they truly love the game, if they would play it anyway—regardless of the money—they can't possibly be considered workaholics. The only descriptive word I could use that fits is FUN-aholic.

The difference? Loving what you do so much that you can't wait to get started and you hate to stop.

We all love doing lots of things that fit that definition. For most of us, however, that would *not* describe what we do for a living. I'm going to show you, in this book, exact steps you can take to turn whatever it is you love doing most into a profit-generating small business, fully capable of paying you a fat second salary that can, with the proper application of the steps I will show you, eventually earn you more money than you make now at a regular, less fun, full-time job.

Even better, you'll be able to turn those things you enjoy doing most into a tax write-off through your new business. This can easily make your fun—the things you most enjoy doing—*free*.

I hear the skeptic in you rearing its ugly head and starting to howl in disbelief. I'm not offended. It's just all those years of being taught differently, struggling to remain true to the erroneous vision of life that you were led to believe.

Don't worry. It's true. You don't need to write *anything* to make my system work for you. If you *do* write, you'll love the process I'm going to take you through—and you'll finally start making money with your writing like you've never seen before—without *ever* receiving another rejection slip again.

A BEST-SELLING AUTHOR'S LIFE—WITHOUT WRITING A WORD

Of course, writing *is* involved in my process—it's just not required that you do any of it to churn out loads of high-quality, interesting, and compelling information people will want to buy from you.

I've been blessed. I love to read and write. I've spent most of my life writing and publishing, applying both to my most passionate interests. The result has always been either free fun—or free fun plus FUN Money. Every time.

But, today, thanks to my system, you don't need to enjoy or excel at either to have a blast doing what I've always done.

When I was sixteen, for example, I loved being the rebel. The turbulent late 1960s and early 1970s had a strong hold on me, and I was determined to spit in the face of "the man" any way I could. So—I launched a small underground newspaper for my school. In it, I pointed out the stupidity of the administration and encouraged other students to stop letting themselves be pushed around.

It's odd, really. For some reason, I got to see the inside of the principal's office a *lot* during that period of my life. But, I learned early on that the right to a free press is one of our most powerful, most protected rights as citizens of the United States. The administration screamed at me and threatened me. But they couldn't legally force me to stop.

To an overly rebellious hormone-driven seventeen-year-old hippie wannabe from Kansas, the notoriety was *heaven.*

I never really made any money publishing that paper, but it was the most fun I ever had in school, and I caught the attention of a *lot* of girls—which was even better than money to me, at the time.

Later, I figured out I could apply writing and publishing to anything I loved doing and, eventually, turn it into money. At the very least, I found ways to turn my writing and publishing into all kinds of free stuff I couldn't otherwise afford to buy for myself.

Free Video Games—And More

When Atari released the 2600—one of the first cartridge-based video game consoles, all I could say was—"Wow!" For the first time that I knew of, you could buy new games and take on challenges that were considerably more engaging than simply batting a square back and forth over an on-screen net. I loved those machines. But, I didn't have much money.

At the time, I was married with children, playing househusband at home, and working on my writing and publishing whenever the children were taking naps, at school, or after they went to bed. Money to buy video game cartridges was out of the question.

I launched *The Logical Gamer,* a printed tabloid-size newsletter for people who loved these games like I did, but couldn't afford to simply buy every new cartridge that came out. I wrote to the manufacturers of the games for all the game consoles, requesting review copies for the newsletter. They responded by sending box after box after box of new games—many of them prerelease. Some were mere chips soldered onto a board that would barely slide into the game slot—true prototypes.

This was pre-online. Before the dial-up computer bulletin boards that predate the World Wide Web by more than 10 years—and before word processors were affordable, I had to type out every issue on an IBM Selectric typewriter twice—once to count the letters in each column, then once again, to add spacing to create justified columns. Then, I had to coat the backs of each column with hot wax and paste them carefully on layout sheets, which were mailed to a printer.

Still, I loved every minute of it. UPS was pulling up to my door daily. It was like Christmas year-round, ripping those packages open to see what new toys had arrived. It was fun work—and the payoff, in my mind, was tremendous.

Lucky you! You're discovering my process after all the *work* has been taken out of it. The system I'm going to show you in this book holds more power than what I did back then, with far less work that is much easier and much more fun to do. And the cost is minimal by comparison.

The Logical Gamer was my first attempt at making money doing something I loved doing for fun. I did make a little money—until the leading newsstand video game magazine of the time launched *its* exclusive video game review newsletter and killed mine in the process. But that's another story.

Personal computers were just hitting the scene, and I needed one to manage the growing list of subscribers I was building for my newsletter.

That's when I discovered all the other things a computer could also help me with—including word processing, typesetting, and connecting to the world.

Moving through the learning curve required switching from using a typewriter to using a word processor, I was at a Radio Shack one day and saw something called a modem. This modem thing, the clerk told me, enabled me to hook my computer up to a telephone line, dial out, and actually *connect* with *another computer.*

I told the clerk that sounded intriguing—unless no one else out there has modems on their computers to connect to.

That clerk changed my life forever. He told me, "There are hundreds of people running computer bulletin boards (BBSs) that you can dial into right now, to exchange messages with other people who dial in, download games and software. I think there are two or three right here in Topeka, Kansas."

I bought the modem and discovered a fascinating "underworld" I never knew existed.

Soon, I launched a publication called *INFO-MAT* and started distributing it online, to the people who operated BBSs. Each BBS was connected to one or more telephone lines. You had to dial in over the phone lines to access them. You could do almost anything on a BBS that you're probably used to doing on the Web today—but you had to dial your local BBS to do it, or rack up *enormous* long distance charges dialing BBSs outside of your local calling area to do them.

Again—lucky you! Now we have the World Wide Web, which easily takes the system I'm going to show you into the realm of possibility for anyone willing to follow the simple steps that are involved.

INFO-MAT was a weekly review of news of interest to computer owners. I sold it, syndication-style, to independent operators of BBSs (called sysops—short for system operator) with an exclusivity agreement that would lock out competitors in their local calling area—as long as the sysop continued paying his or her monthly bill.

Few ever missed a payment—and the network grew. I had finally discovered a way to start earning *real* money from my passion—technology, computers—through writing and publishing. I actually started paying myself a salary and could tell people this was now my job—even though I was still having a blast every minute of every day doing it.

Free Music, Too

Then, compact discs were born. I fell in love all over again.

I've always been a big fan of music—mostly rock and blues, but also almost every other category imaginable. Unfortunately, the more I listened to my albums, the more I destroyed them. CDs were amazing to me and I wanted to build a huge collection. Sadly, although I was now earning a salary from BBS Press Service, Inc. (the company I formed to publish *INFO-MAT*), I still wasn't making enough to squander on anything but the occasional CD. I wanted more.

Online Digital Music Review was born.

I dashed off letters to all the major record labels, requesting that they put me on their review lists. About two weeks later, I got a call from Warner Brothers. The lady on the other end of the line worked in their publicity office. I thought, "Okay, here comes the letdown."

Instead, she asked, "Did you *really* want to receive review copies of *all* the CDs we release, regardless of the category?"

I swallowed and, without hesitation, said, "Yes—I do. We intend to review all types of music."

"You do realize we publish roughly 75 percent of all the music released in the world today?"

"I do now," I said. "And I still want them." I held my breath, waiting for the inevitable letdown I just knew was coming.

"Okay," she said. "We've added you to the list."

The other labels didn't even bother to call—they just started shipping me all their new releases. UPS was back at my door daily, and I was in seventh heaven.

There is a lot more. I've now repeated the process countless times, for ever-increasing amounts of money—but I don't want to bore you with all the details here. Instead, I know you want to focus on setting up *your* FUN Money system. The point is, I now realize that, barring a short stint in the job market, I've always looked to my own passions and interests and created a source of revenue out of them, through publishing. In short, I've always been a hopeless FUNahaolic!

And I haven't held a "real job," working for someone else, since I was 25.

I hope you can see clearly now that, regardless of your interests, whatever it is that "turns you on" and sets your creative juices flowing can be turned into cash, thanks to the system I'm going to spell out for you in this book.

Luckily, you live in an age where the Internet makes it possible to create a business built completely around the things you find most fun—*and* make money doing them, spending very little money to get started and seeing results almost right away.

I can't guarantee that following the steps in this book will ever earn you rock-star money—but I do guarantee you'll discover how easy it is to live a rock-star life, enjoying what you do for fun so much you never feel like you're working to make money again.

I can also guarantee it's much easier than you think it is. All you need is access to a computer, a rudimentary understanding of the Web, and some experience with word processing or a willingness to learn—and you can do it.

You don't even need to know how to write.

Even if you're an accomplished writer, I'm going to encourage you to start thinking like a publisher because this is where the *real* money is. This is what will pull you out of the "do what you love and *hope* the money follows" mode, and take you straight to the "turn *everything* you love doing most into money" mode, the quickest, easiest way possible.

PUBLISHERS MAKE THE REAL MONEY

Think about it: Publishers, generally speaking, always make more money than the authors who actually write what they publish.

Renowned science fiction author Isaac Asimov, who still holds the unchallenged Guinness World Record for the most books written by a single author, couldn't churn out as much material as a publisher can because publishers don't have to actually write the works they publish. The number and variety of books a publisher can churn out each year is limited only by the market's desire to buy what they publish. Isaac Asimov still had to operate within limits that publishers simply don't have. He was a virtual writing machine in human form—but he was still limited to the number of words he could write in any given day.

A publisher can work with hundreds of authors. *Some* authors make huge money—but their publishers get a cut of *all* of the author's earnings. To make more money, they simply have to find more authors. While there are only so many books a single author can create in any given year, there are an almost infinite number of books that can be *published*.

I'm going to show you how to become an online publisher and launch an online business that *erases* those limitations for you, too. Then, in the process, we'll use your newfound skill to erase *all* the limitations from your life.

Prepare yourself. You're about to become a FUNaholic. After reading this book, you'll be fully loaded up and ready to start enjoying all the hours of fun you can imagine, living a life that's so profitable you'll wonder why you waited so long to get started. The good news is: It's never too late to get going.

My name is Alan, and I'm a FUNaholic.

Say "Hello, Alan," and let's get rolling!

ABOUT THE AUTHOR

You're going to get to know me very well by the time you've read this book. I don't want to risk boring you twice, so I'll keep this short.

I've had publishing in my veins ever since I was in the third grade. I've also developed a love of writing—but it's information publishing that I've always enjoyed most. I've developed and discovered dozens of shortcuts through the years. These shortcuts led me to my simple three-step system.

I've tested the system repeatedly with great—often stellar—results almost every time. Every time the results were off even slightly, I adjusted my system. For more than 23 years.

You now hold that system in your hands. I'm pleased you purchased this book. So is Carol. Also the BBS Press Service, Inc. staff—and the IRS. It might sound trite for me to say, but it's honestly more important to me that you apply what I've provided to you here. I've always turned what I love doing most into money. I haven't held a full-time job for 30 years, but I still vividly remember the experience of working for someone else. It's much worse if what you're doing for someone else isn't what you truly enjoy spending your time doing.

The system you now hold in your hands has been honed and refined through many years of hard trial and error. The result is a method that works. It's stood the test of time. And it's been simplified to the point of connect-the-dots adaptability.

It's very simple to follow the simple three-step formula as it stands today. Now there is no reason you should avoid giving it a try. Let me hear about your results. I'm always on the lookout for more FUN Money people to profile.

If you benefit from this book and would like to know even more of what I know and continue to learn, please check out my Ticket to Wealth Gold Level program on www.FUNdamentalYou.com.

CHAPTER 1

THE SITCOM AS LIFE

Unless each day can be looked back upon by an individual as one in which he has had some fun, some joy, some real satisfaction, that day is a loss.

—Anonymous

WHY YOUR LIFE NEVER MATCHES WHAT YOU SEE ON THE SCREEN—AND HOW EASY IT IS TO CREATE A LIFE THAT DOES

Close your eyes and imagine along with me.

Wait a minute. I just remembered. You're *reading* this. You'd better keep your eyes open. It's kind of hard reading with your eyes closed.

Back up. Rewind and edit.

Read along and imagine with me. Ask yourself as you read—does the following scene sound familiar?

Fade in.

The office is humming with activity. Everywhere you look in the large, overly lit room, people sit in cubicles, industriously typing, talking on the phone, and examining computer screens.

Quickly, we swing into one cubicle for a close-up. The rest of the office blurs and fades away while the sound of office activity softens to a background hum.

In the cubicle that comes into view, a young, slender, cherry-blonde woman sits looking at eBay on her computer. She snaps her chewing gum while she does her nails. In her cubicle, every surface but the desk and two office chairs is covered with Barbie dolls, Barbie doll posters, Barbie doll books, and Barbie doll accessories.

As we watch, she tries without success to match the rhythm of her gum chewing to the strokes of her nail file. She tries alternating the beats, then tries to match the rhythm.

Suddenly, she takes the gum out of her mouth. Clearly frustrated, still holding her gum in one hand, she looks around on her desk for a place to put it. Her desk is covered with paperwork. Frowning, she starts to stick the gum first on one stack of papers, then on another.

Finally, she shoves several stacks of paper aside, places her gum firmly on the desk, then quickly shuffles some papers back over it.

She taps something on her computer keyboard. Then she clenches her fists, staring intently at the screen.

"Damn."

She types quickly again. Then she sits, staring in anticipation.

"Damn."

"Jenny?"

The voice catches her by surprise. Jenny jumps a good foot out of her chair, spins, and sees her friend, Tom, standing in the doorway to her cubicle. He's smiling mischievously.

"Don't you *ever* knock, Tom?" Jenny asks, wide-eyed. "You scared the living daylights out of me."

"There's no door on these cubicles, Jenny. C'mon. What good would knocking do?"

Tom steps into Jenny's cubicle and plops down in one of the two empty chairs, swinging his feet up to rest on the seat of the unoccupied chair. "Are you still looking for that Barbie you've been blathering about for months?"

"Yeah," Jenny says. "I'm still lookin'." She stares intently at the screen again. Then, she taps a few keys and sits, watching the screen.

"Damn. I can't believe it, Tom. This is the first time I've seen a genuine side-parted bubble-cut Barbie on eBay in *months*—and *somebody* out there keeps outbidding me the moment I bid it up. Crap. I'd gladly give a month's salary for that Barbie."

Tom laughs. "I'd give a full year's salary to anyone who can explain why you'd want another Barbie at all."

Another voice pipes up at the cubicle door. "Me, too."

Jenny and Tom both jump nearly a foot, in unison, snapping their startled attention to the doorway. It's Jenny and Tom's mutual friend, Albert.

"Why don't you just make your top bid a full month's salary?" Albert asks. "Then the system will place the next highest bid for you automatically. That'll make it tougher for anyone to outbid you so quickly."

Wearing thick-rimmed glasses, a white shirt not all the way tucked in, and a black pencil-thin tie, Albert laughs nervously, ending with a loud snort.

"Albert," Jenny says, composing herself. "I can't afford to spend a month's salary, no matter how badly I'd love to add that Barbie to my collection. That was just a figure of speech. Besides—it's more fun actually bidding on them."

"Either way, I'm with Tom," Albert replies. "I can't imagine why any adult would want *one* Barbie, let alone hundreds."

Jenny looks perturbed. "I don't have *hundreds* of Barbies. For cryin' out loud. Everybody knows Barbie's special. She was a part of my childhood. I grew up with her. She's—like—my *role model*. And the side-parted bubble-cut Barbie is one of the only truly rare Barbies I still don't have."

As Albert enters the cubicle, Tom sits up, taking his feet off the only other chair in the cramped space. Albert slumps into the now-open chair, his posture slouched.

Smiling again, Tom says, "There, there, Jenny. We understand. I'm sure your life won't be complete without her."

Jenny stares solemnly at Tom for a minute. "You're mocking me. You really don't understand. After all the time we've worked together and known each other, you still don't get it, do you?"

Both Tom and Albert speak in unison ... deadpan serious. They shake their heads back and forth in unison. "Actually ... we don't."

Tom says, "I have to admit it, but Matchbox cars were my favorite toy when I was a kid. I'd even have to say they were important to me during that time. But, I still don't feel the slightest pressure to have every Matchbox car ever manufactured during my childhood today."

Albert chortles, pushing his glasses up, which slide back down on his nose with each shoulder-shaking snicker. "Hah. That's the truth, Tom. Now you collect *live* Barbies instead."

Tom smirks at Albert. "What's your point, smart-ass? I'd much rather have a living, breathing Barbie in my room than something made out of plastic. And—no—it doesn't count if she's inflatable."

Albert waves Tom away, blushing.

Jenny scowls at both of them. "You two are so *clueless*. Barbie means everything to me. I collect her. I care about her and think about her all the time. I can't wait to clock out and spend time with my collection. I'm happiest when I'm trading online with other collectors, and looking for the few missing dolls that I still need."

"You're right—we're clueless." Tom and Albert speak in unison again. Laughing, they throw up their hands in mock exasperation.

Jenny snaps her attention around, back to the screen, then points at it. "Damn. See? You two pop in here, distract me, and I lost the auction." She turns to look disapprovingly back at the two young men, still sitting in her cubicle. "You guys made me miss it. It's *your* fault."

Another voice breaks in from the cubicle doorway. "I understand *completely*, Jenny."

This time, Jenny, Tom, and Albert all jump at the sound, snapping their heads in the direction of the doorway in unison. Their mutual friend, Gloria, a slightly pudgy brunette with long, flowing hair and a pretty face, stands there, leaning against the glass.

"It's like my Corvette fetish, Jenny. I *love* Corvettes. I'd do *anything* to get one of my own."

Tom gives an exaggerated nod. "I know, Gloria. You've been known to do *anything* just to *ride* in one."

Albert and Tom laugh uproariously. Jenny suppresses a chuckle of her own behind a hand. Gloria frowns disapprovingly.

"No—really," Gloria says. "Jenny loves Barbies. I love Corvettes. Tom loves easy women. Albert loves ... whatever it is Albert loves. So what? It gives us all something to work toward, something to look forward to. It gives us a reason to come in here, work nine-to-five, struggle to please a stupid boss, and put up with all the hassles of life. That's good—right?" She nods, smiling, at each of the other three in unison. Jenny smiles back. Tom and Albert wave Gloria away, skeptical.

"You guys will never understand," Gloria says.

"You got that right," Jenny chimes in.

Gloria changes the subject. "So—what are you guys planning to do tonight?"

Another voice booms from behind Gloria, almost growling, "How about all four of you getting some work done before you worry about what you're doing tonight?"

Jenny, Tom, Albert, and Gloria all jump in unison at the sound. Behind Gloria, a tall, balding, heavy-set fellow stands, hands on hips, a scowl planted on his face.

Tom and Albert jump up instinctively, then bustle around the cubicle, bumping into each other as they try to get through the door Gloria is still blocking. They stop moments before colliding with her.

"Sure, boss," Jenny says, quickly closing the eBay window on her computer and typing furiously on the word processor that sat right behind eBay on the screen. "We were just . . . exchanging some facts."

"Uh . . . thanks for helping straighten out that discrepancy, Jenny," Tom says, nervously, jumping up from his chair to head toward the door.

He steps first to the left, then to the right, at the same time as Gloria steps to the left, then right, until it looks like he'll never get past her. He's obviously desperate to scurry back to his own cubicle.

Gloria finally turns to leave. Tom pops out the opening behind her, then sidesteps the boss, to slip away as Albert approaches the cubicle opening, still under the boss' watchful eye.

"Hi, boss—see ya, Jenny."

"See ya, Albert," Jenny says. Still trying to look busy, she quickly grabs one of her misplaced stacks of papers and sets it directly on top of the other papers she'd laid over the wad of gum earlier. Now the gum is hopelessly stuck to her desk—but at least it's hidden from sight.

As the boss enters her cubicle, Jenny absent-mindedly pats the papers down, cementing them and the gum to her desk even more.

Fade out.

Life Isn't *Really* like This . . . Is It?

Does this sound like your life? It might sound slightly familiar, but different, too. You might lose your job if you were caught doing what Jenny, Tom, Albert, and Gloria were doing—wouldn't you? At the very least, you'd probably catch a lot more flack from your boss than their boss gave to them.

The scene I just painted is eerily familiar because, at work, we're constantly thinking about what we really enjoy doing—*if* our work isn't the source of that joy in the first place. Unfortunately, far too few of us ever land the kind of job that's truly fun and liberating. We can't all work for Google, so most of our lives are burned up churning the hours necessary to pay the bills and trying to find time to enjoy *some* of the hours that remain when we clock out.

I'm going to change all of that for you through the simple system I'll lay out in the chapters that lie ahead.

First, tell me—would you agree that the previous scene sounds more like a sitcom than your life? Could this be the source of any familiar feelings you might have had as you read that scene?

If that's what you felt, you're right on target. Just insert a laugh track and the scene we described could easily fit into a dozen different television sitcoms.

I'm sure you've seen at least a few. Come on—we're friends now that you bought this book. Admit it. Most of us have seen more sitcoms than we care to admit. And, if we're truly honest with ourselves, most of us would love to have a job like the ones we see on these shows, if such a job actually existed.

But—have you ever noticed how rarely it is that these shows resemble *real life?*

At work, sitcom characters spend virtually all their time working on personal matters. They discuss what happened at home last night. They gossip about the other employees. They pull pranks and joke with each other constantly.

On rare occasions, they might even get into competitions with some of the other employees. Usually, it's about who can sell the most Girl Scout cookies or who can stick the most pencils into the ceiling fastest—nothing to do with the actual work they're being paid to perform. But, at least there's a sense of purpose and drive involved in the activity.

On these shows, the boss is also almost always a background character, scowling, unhappy with the productivity of his workers, but also never pushed to the point of firing anyone.

After all, firing someone, or even *requiring* people in the office to get something productive done, would kill the buzz on a sitcom. In these shows, the boss is usually either a bungling idiot, oblivious to the lack of productive work going on around him and part of the problem himself, or a scowling straight man trying desperately to keep his employees working, but without a clue when it comes to motivating them to actually accomplish anything.

Sitcoms are, after all, about *comedy*. They're *supposed* to be funny and—let's be honest—actual work isn't usually perceived as being much fun.

...Or—is it?

I want to show you how much fun work—even *hard* work—can be. All you need to do is find the *right* work to do, then discover how to make it pay.

Ask yourself: does *any* sitcom you've *ever* seen match your life?

It's Never Been like a Sitcom for Me

I've only held a few "real" jobs in my life, but I can safely say none of them were anything like the jobs I've seen on sitcoms.

One boss I had furiously smoked a pipe. *All day*. He would use his pipe to literally fume when you didn't have the right answers to his questions. I swear I heard his pipe bit crack whenever he was seriously pissed, which generally worked out to be most of the time.

This guy must have spent a huge percentage of his inflated salary on new pipe bits.

Many times, this wretched soul was pissed at me. Most of the time, it didn't matter whether he was angry or not. The guy not only ran the company—he was also out on the street, bringing in sales. If he had a bad day out selling, he'd storm into the office, throw things, and then stomp around yelling at everyone, regardless of how busy we were.

He was likeable enough when things were going perfectly. But, those times were extremely rare.

One day, after hitting the streets for several hours without making any sizeable sales, this guy (notice how I hesitate to call him "boss") stormed through the building to his office and slammed the door. We all listened intently as he slammed and banged things around behind that closed door for a while. And—we looked at each other in silence, braced for the worst.

When his office door swung open again, we immediately dropped our eyes back to the work before us and focused on our tasks, praying we could somehow avoid his gaze as he stormed into our area.

I wasn't so lucky.

Even though I was working diligently at the far end of the room, in spite of the fact that this man wasn't actually mad at *me*, he asked another employee about the status of a job we were working on—and didn't get the answer he wanted to hear at that moment.

In anger, he grabbed an X-Acto knife and hurled it across the room. I heard the knife whiz past my ear. It was *that* close. The blade stuck into the wall I was facing with a loud "thwang," directly in front of me. Then, without a word, the guy turned around and stomped back into his office, slamming the door behind him.

All activity in the office froze. Nobody said a word. Nobody breathed. I kept waiting for the laugh track to kick in, but it never happened. Maybe I was too stunned to hear it. Maybe this was real life, instead.

Looking at that knife in the wall, I realized I'd just narrowly escaped being *stabbed* by this jerk—and I immediately walked out the door. I hopped in my car and drove directly to the unemployment office, where I made a claim, based on the fact that my boss had just thrown an X-Acto knife at me.

Luckily, the unemployment claim was granted. I didn't feel like immediately going out looking for another job right then.

I don't know about you, but I've never worked in *any* job where three or more of us were allowed to gather for anything besides a general staff meeting without catching a bunch of guff from a supervisor or boss who would gleefully inform us all that we're "just this close" to being fired.

The threat was usually so pronounced that no one would think for a minute of hanging out and chatting. My bosses routinely reminded me that I was easily replaceable and, if I didn't want to work, I could quit right now.

Was I cursed? Did some bizarre permutation of the universe lead me to only apply and get hired for jobs in the worst possible places to work?

I don't think so. I'll bet at least some of you have had jobs that are more like the one I did. You might be working at one today.

Personal Time—On the Clock

Anyway—there are perhaps at least *some* similarities between your work life and the jobs you see in sitcoms. You probably *think* about personal business while you're working, whenever that's reasonably possible. If you're like almost everyone else, you probably start out each day fresh, get into your work flow and, after 5 or 10 minutes, start watching the clock—eager for quitting time to come, so you can go home and start *living*.

Even if you already own your own business, chances are it's not at all like the businesses we see people running in sitcoms. If you ran things like a sitcom entrepreneur, your business would go up in flames. Revenue would come to a screeching halt. You'd have lots of laughs—but there wouldn't be a business to run after a while.

It makes sense, when you think about it. We tune in to sitcoms to have fun. Work is rarely perceived as having anything to do with fun. Therefore, anything even resembling real work simply doesn't play well as entertainment.

Sadly, real work is a part of real life. You have to pay the bills and the mortgage and buy groceries or life itself gets a *lot* less fun.

If life was more like it appears on the sitcoms, we'd all be happier. But we wouldn't have enough money to actually *do* anything fun in the short time we have when we're *not* at work because the companies we worked for would self-destruct if they were run like sitcom companies. Then, there wouldn't be *any* place to work to earn a living.

Never fear—I'm going to tell you how to make all the money you want to make, have fun doing it, and enjoy every minute of the work you do to make more than enough money to survive. You can, at a minimum, utilize the simple system I'll show you to more than cover the cost of what you already love doing most. With some patience and effort, you can even replace your current income and start living like you're already retired.

First, I need to have you answer another personal question (even though I'm speaking these words in your head at the moment, I won't actually hear your answer—so go ahead and be honest):

How's your home life? Is *this* where all those sitcoms finally converge with reality? See if the next scene is at all familiar:

Fade in.

We're in the living room of a small apartment, one week later. The apartment is neat, decorated in a feminine style. Barbie dolls sit in a neat line across the fireplace mantel. There are more Barbies bunched on the two end tables on each side of the overstuffed couch. Not surprisingly, even the artwork on the walls is mostly framed Barbie posters and magazine covers featuring the beloved plastic personality.

Jenny moves from doll to doll, whispering to them as she straightens their hair, fluffs the ruffles on their dresses, or poses them, then repositions their poses—one by one.

The doorbell rings. She jumps, startled, knocking two Barbies to the floor in the process. She stoops quickly and gently picks up each doll, muttering under her breath.

"Sorry. I didn't mean to hurt you." And, "You okay, dear? I'm *so* sorry."

Then, she races to the door and swings it open, revealing her three friends from work—Gloria, Tom, and Albert. They stand with arms open wide. Tom has flowers in his hands and Gloria and Albert each hold gaily wrapped oblong packages.

As the door swings open, they all shout, in unison, "Happy Birthday, Jenny!"

"You guys!" she gushes. "You didn't have to do this for me." Jenny invites them in, waving to the couch.

"Oh—but we did," Tom says, with a devilish grin. "You'd make life at work a living hell if we forgot your birthday."

"Oh, Tom." Jenny says. "I'm not that bad and you *know* it. Thanks for the flowers—they're beautiful."

Jenny quickly removes the flowers from Tom's hand and moves to the kitchenette, to find a vase.

Albert smiles and says, "You're right, Jenny. After all—it's Mr. Noggin's job to make our lives at work miserable—not yours. Open my present first."

Jenny fills the vase, puts the flowers in, fluffs them a bit, then moves back around to the living room area. She sits across from the threesome, seated on the couch, reaches for Albert's present and rips into it quickly, tossing the paper in every direction. As she tears the package open, her eyes brighten and she gets visibly excited, wriggling in her chair.

Once the wrapping is off and the present is fully revealed, she holds it up to the light, a slightly puzzled look on her face that she quickly replaces with a forced smile.

Inside the box is a doll that looks a *lot* like a Barbie—but clearly isn't one.

"Thank you, Albert—uh—what is she, exactly?"

"You don't know?" Albert asks. "It's Tess, the new completely computerized, fully programmable doll from Peach Computers. You can program her to say whatever you want her to say, set timers to make her say them—and you can even set up responses, so she can actually answer spoken questions."

"She's . . . lovely, Albert," Jenny says, reaching across to lay a hand on his arm. "Thank you. I know she'll be fun."

Gloria is frowning. "Albert—Jenny collects *Barbie* dolls . . . not just dolls."

Albert puffs out his chest and replies, "Hey—this is the most technologically advanced doll I've ever seen. All the high-tech magazines are raving about her. I thought she could keep Jenny's other dolls company."

"She's wonderful, Albert," Jenny says, trying to smooth things over. "I'll treasure her because she came from you."

Albert looks down at the floor, blushing visibly, while Jenny shoots Gloria a nasty glare.

Oblivious to Jenny's disapproval, Gloria says, "Open mine next."

Jenny rips open the box, similar in shape and size to the one Albert gave her. This time, she's more reserved, bracing herself for whatever might be inside, unwilling to let her emotions fool her again.

But—as the wrapping comes off, also tossed to the floor with wild abandon, Jenny can't contain herself. Inside is a mint condition side-parted bubble-cut Barbie—just like the one she's been obsessing about and was trying to purchase on eBay earlier that week at work.

"Oh . . . my . . . *God*, Gloria! You found her. You found my dream Barbie. In *perfect* condition. How on earth . . . ?"

Gloria waves her hand dismissively and says, "I almost didn't get her. I found her on eBay, but some fool kept trying to outbid me until I almost gave up. I had no idea there were *other* people who collect Barbies the way you do."

Jenny gasps, breathless. "That was *you?*"

Gloria looks confused.

"I'm that 'fool' who was trying to outbid you. I guess it's a good thing I gave up when I did."

All four friends laugh.

"Hey—I'm glad it worked out the way it did," Gloria said, smiling. "I was afraid you'd find one before I did, and I'd wind up stuck with a toy I gave up playing with years ago."

"I get it, Gloria," Tom says, smiling and winking mischievously. "You've switched from one kind of toy to another. How's your collection of vibrating toys coming along?"

"You cut that out." Jenny yells, mockingly. "Gloria's done something amazing, and all you can do is abuse her for your own amusement. But—seriously—you are *all* amazing. Thank you *so much* for making this birthday truly special."

They all smile and hug.

Gloria speaks up. "Hey—it's not over by a long shot. Eight AM is a long way off. Let's hit the streets and party."

They all nod, smiling, and head out the door. As she's pulling the door closed behind her, Jenny takes one last look at the new, super-rare addition to her collection, now sitting on the couch as if she were alive, waiting patiently for her new owner to return.

"See you soon, princess," Jenny whispers through the door. Then she pulls the door closed and locks it behind her.

Fade out.

Now we've had a chance to see what home life is like for the four unlikely heroes I've introduced to you. It was still kind of sitcom-pretty, wasn't it?

Again, add a laugh track, a few commercial breaks and—it's a prime-time show.

You might have noticed that the lives of Jenny, Tom, Albert, and Gloria, as I've depicted them here, are pretty much the same at home as they are at work.

They all pretty much focus on what they want to do and enjoy doing the most. There was no housecleaning or laundry being done at Jenny's. Not while we were watching, anyway. Her idea of "straightening up" was rearranging her prized collection of Barbie dolls.

Filling a vase with water and putting Tom's flowers in it was about the toughest "job" I saw Jenny tackle during the entire scene.

You're Really Not in Kansas Any More

It still felt slightly familiar, didn't it? But, something's not quite right. Jenny lives in a neat apartment and spends all her spare time tidying up her dolls, studying them, and looking for new additions to her collection—but she tosses gift wrapping on the floor with wild abandon, ignoring it as she heads out the door with her friends.

In *our* world, we might tuck that gift wrap neatly into the trash after we unwrapped our presents—or we would at least pick it all up before we left (well—most of us would. I understand some of you wouldn't throw the paper away—but your home wouldn't be as neat as Jenny's).

Jenny clearly isn't worried about it, either way. Maybe she decided to pick it up later, when she returns home from her celebration with her friends—but it's nowhere to be seen when she takes that last loving glance back at her latest acquisition, on the way out the door.

Was it magic?

Yes. Sort of. It's the magic of fiction, brought to life and delivered to your home as television entertainment in written form.

Again, it wouldn't be entertaining if it included all the mundane chores and day-to-day rituals we all go through as part of our ordinary, nontelevised lives. I defy you to find many routine everyday tasks like taking out the trash, scrubbing the tub, or doing dishes being carried out on television shows of *any* kind—even the glorified game shows so many people refer to as "reality" TV today.

It simply doesn't happen because these shows are something we turn to, to take us *away* from the mundane, everyday reality we usually have to face, just to pay the bills and keep up the appearance that we're civilized beings who care about our surroundings

What You *Never* See on Television

You won't find much of this stuff on television or in the movies or in the books we read—because we're looking for entertainment from these sources. We want our entertainment to be fun—and work of any kind simply doesn't fall under the classification of "fun" for most people.

I'm pretty certain you feel, like most people do, that work is something you do to get the money you need to pay your rent and bills and buy groceries. Fun is something you do with whatever time and money you have left after paying all your bills.

I'm right, aren't I?

Sadly, most people who make enough money to really enjoy the fun things in life work so many hours that there's no time left to have much fun. And, most people with lots of time for fun don't make enough money to really enjoy the additional time for fun that they do have.

It's a serious Catch-22 that, at first, seems impossible to break through. So, most people go through life working at a job they don't really enjoy, trading away the bulk of their lives for the dollars they believe are necessary to cover expenses, stealing away just an hour here or an hour there to really enjoy life.

The point is—this second scene probably didn't sound any more like your *life* than the first scene sounded like your *job*. Did it?

I didn't think so.

There is a way out, and I'm here to tell you how it's done. Even better—it's not nearly as difficult as you might imagine, although some attitude adjustments are in order if you're ever going to truly succeed in making this all work for you.

All you need to do is look at work in a different way, and every waking moment of your life can be like living in a sitcom or being on vacation for life, with more money pouring in than you could ever make working at a regular, real-life job again.

Suspend your disbelief long enough to try the steps I'll show you. I am certain you'll agree.

Remember—you weren't at all skeptical when Jenny's birthday wrapping miraculously disappeared from her apartment floor just a while ago. You didn't even think about it. Just do the same as you read the rest of this book. I'm really not going to ask anything of you that's more difficult than you can handle.

INVENTORYING YOUR LIFE EXPERIENCE

This book is about starting a business to turn your favorite pastimes into money. It's truly possible to do what you enjoy doing most *all* the time, earn a living doing it, and never look back on the job world again—*if* you follow the steps I'll be outlining as we move forward. Worst-case, you'll start enjoying your free time more, because it'll be paid for and tax deductible. Like all fun should be.

We'll get to the nuts and bolts of starting that business and how to easily turn it into a profitable enterprise, possibly moving into it full-time, in a minute.

First, you need to take a long, hard look at your life. That's why I started things off with those two scenes. (I know as well as you do that you don't need more sitcoms.)

What I'm suggesting is an intervention, of sorts. Not the kind where you get locked in a room while all the people in your life who truly care about you hammer you with the reality of your current situation, long enough that you see it for yourself.

I'm reasonably certain you've done a pretty good job of hammering yourself most of your life if you're like most of the clients I work with on a day-by-day basis.

Instead, I'm inviting you to ease into this in a much gentler way. For the sake of clarity, I'll call this process a *gentle*vention.

Sitcom Role Models?

Jenny, Tom, Albert, and Gloria are great role models for you. I revealed their stories here so that I could bring their experiences to life for you. Through the process you'll be following throughout the rest of this book, you'll eventually be joining them.

No—you won't have to collect Barbie dolls like Jenny does or living Barbies, like it would appear Tom does (unless, of course, that's what you *really* love doing). And there won't be any need for you to learn to love tech gadgets like Albert does or long to own Corvettes like Gloria does, either (unless, again, that's something you truly do love).

But, eventually, you should find one of these four fictional people that you can relate to. Chances are good you already resonated with one. We'll be focusing on Jenny throughout most of the book—but I'll eventually bring it all back around at the end, so you can see how this works out for each of the characters we've come to know together.

You don't have to decide now. I'll help you with that soon. Enough.

It All Starts with a List or Two

For now, I want you to take out a sheet of paper or open up a fresh document in your word processor. Then, I want you to list 10 things you've done in your past that you truly enjoyed doing, so much you could easily spend all your waking moments doing them.

You should list 10 items. Most people find it easy to come up with five favorite activities fairly quickly. The other five usually require a bit more digging. The digging is worth the effort. Your second group of five favorite activities could well be the gold we're mining for here.

Leave nothing off the list, regardless of how silly or mundane it might seem. Even things you've only done once, a long time ago.

If *you* enjoyed it and would love doing it more often, it's important to include it on your list.

Yes, sex can go on the list (I told you I couldn't hear you thinking— but I heard you that time). But—only add it to your list if you could handle doing something related to sex all the time, day in, day out. Pun unintended.

Be honest. Most everyone I know enjoys sex. But—all day, every day? Whew. I've never put it on my list because I can't imagine filling my days with . . . well, you get the picture.

Still—if that's really what you love doing, put it on the list. No one will read this list but you (and I really can't hear what you're thinking—that last one was a trick), so write it down if it's something you love doing, and you're sure you would like to do it more often, even for a living.

Here's Jenny's list, to help you see what I mean:

- Reading
- Shopping
- Sewing
- Listening to R&B classics
- Watching romantic movies
- Collecting Barbie dolls
- Traveling
- Riding horses
- eBay
- Teaching (I taught grade school before I moved to my data-entry job at Global Exterior Shelving.)

Jenny's list isn't in any particular order. Your list doesn't have to be, either. It's also okay if your list doesn't include anything Jenny's list contains. Every activity on your list could be identical to Jenny's, too—if you're being honest about it and that's the way it works out.

I just want your list to be truly *your* list.

It's important to point out that Jenny's list includes three activities she didn't think of at first. Forced to come up with 10 items, she wrote down the first seven quickly, without thinking much about it.

She added teaching, riding horses, and travel after staring at her list of seven items a long while, digging deeper, like I want you to make certain you do, too.

Fun Jobs, Too

I hope you also noticed that your list can contain occupations you really loved or even your current occupation, if you're truly passionate about it and love doing it.

Now—get going. Make that list. I'll see you back here in a few minutes. Take as long as you need. I'm stuck on this page until you return, so I'll just catch up on some reading and listen to some good blues while I wait for you.

Are you done? Good. I enjoyed the break, but I also love working with you so much I'm glad you're ready to continue.

NOTE: If you're one of those people who reads books like this, but never completes the exercises when asked, shame on you. It's okay if you don't want to participate, but I certainly don't want to hear from you later that you read my book and it didn't help you.

I'll also summarize my points and include exercises at the end of each section of this book. Once you've satisfied your curiosity and read the entire book through once, if you're the type who would rather skip the exercises for now, please do yourself a favor, go back through the end of each section and *work* the easy exercises when you've finished your first read. I want you to write me when you've established your FUN Money life, and you really do need to do the simple steps I've outlined to get there.

IDENTIFYING YOUR REAL PASSION

Now—it's time to take a look at your list.

What *single item* on your list have you had the opportunity to do the most often? Rearrange your list, placing the activities you've been doing the least at the bottom and working up the list of 10 or more items, to the one you just identified as something you've done the most.

Remember—we're not looking for those activities you've been doing the longest time. We want to order your list of favorite activities, starting at the top, with the one you've done the most *often*.

Jenny's list, rearranged this way, looks like this:

- Reading
- Collecting Barbie dolls
- Listening to R&B classics

17

- Watching romantic movies
- Shopping
- eBay
- Sewing
- Teaching
- Traveling
- Riding horses

In Jenny's case, she's always loved reading, from the time she was a young girl. She got her first Barbie (which she replaced recently, buying another one exactly like it on eBay) before she could read. But, she reads every chance she gets.

This makes collecting Barbie dolls second on Jenny's list, because she's spent so much time studying them, looking for them, and admiring and caring for her collection through so many years—just not as much time as she's spent reading.

Listening to R&B classics is actually a close tie to collecting Barbies for Jenny. This is one of the items she struggled to discover while making her list. She likes to listen to music and, whenever possible, chooses R&B classics when she does.

Jenny's love of romantic movies came along in her late teens—but she's done a lot to make up for lost time by watching as many as she can, whenever possible. She says they make life as a single woman worth living.

Shopping isn't one of Jenny's *favorite* activities—but she's certainly had a lot of opportunity to shop, and she enjoys it when she does.

These days, when Jenny shops, eBay is her favorite place to be, because she's almost always on the site anyway, looking for rare Barbies, watching what they sell for, studying the descriptions to see if she can find a better example of one doll or another being offered, and noticing who the Barbie doll "power sellers" are.

Jenny took up sewing so she could repair Barbie clothes and, on occasion, make her own. This is another activity she had to think about a while before she added it to her list. She enjoys sewing, but she's truly "in the zone" with her sewing machine when she's working on something for her Barbies.

Jenny's list is rounded out with teaching, travel, and riding horses. She dearly loves all three activities, but she doesn't get the chance to pursue them often. She couldn't afford to live the way she does today on a teacher's salary. Even her new, considerably higher salary at her current job isn't enough to cover the cost of travel very often. And she only got to ride a horse a few times when she was very young.

She would love to have a horse and live on a farm but, in the heart of the city, that's not going to happen any time soon. At least, that's what *she* thinks now.

How do you feel about all the activities on your list? Any similar situations? My own has several, and I'll bet yours does, too.

Soon, I'm going to show you exact steps you can take to focus in on what you love doing the most and to create a lifestyle that allows you to pursue that activity as much as you want, adding a reliable second income in the process and possibly replacing your current income completely.

A Second List Helps Clarify Planning

First, you need to make another list.

Don't worry—I'm not going to do this to you throughout the entire book. I'll do my best to keep it to a minimum—but this is important, right now. Don't complain. Just do it. The potential rewards will be huge.

This is all-important preparatory work. These are steps you must take before implementing my simple three-step formula for maximum results. You could just dive right in—but these steps will help you make certain you're diving into a pool filled with water.

Your second list is more like one you might need for a resume. Each item on this list should be a job you've held in your life. List every job, regardless of how long you held it or how unimportant it might appear at first.

Here's Jenny's list:

- Clothing store clerk
- Third grade teacher
- Assistant School Librarian
- Data-entry clerk
- Candy striper
- Fast food salesclerk

Unlike the other list, your list of jobs you've held can be as long or as short as your work experience happens to be. Don't forget to include volunteer positions—these count as jobs, too.

Jenny put in a stint as a candy striper and enjoyed it, but hospitals make her ill at ease, so she quit after a short while. She also didn't last long as a fast food salesclerk and didn't care for the job at all, but it's still on her list. She only worked at the clothing store during one holiday season rush, but this was her first job ever. She truly loved making her own money and getting a discount on clothes her mother would never have bought for her at the time.

Her stint as an assistant school librarian, also voluntary, ran during her tenure as a teacher. Naturally, she loved it, because she loves teaching and kids and books, and she considered it perfect—even better than teaching, in many ways. But, it paid almost nothing.

Today, she's a data-entry clerk. She doesn't like it at all, but the pay is good, and she sees it as necessary.

I'll wake Jenny out of this self-inflicted trance soon. You, too.

First, reorder your list, putting your *favorite* job at the top. Then, work through to the bottom, where your least favorite should go.

Jenny's re-ordered list looks like this:

- Third grade teacher
- Assistant school librarian
- Clothing store clerk
- Candy striper
- Data-entry clerk
- Fast food salesclerk

Now that you're getting to know Jenny a bit better, the reordering she did on this list is fairly self-explanatory.

Notice, the *only* job she disliked more than the job she holds today is working the register in a fast food restaurant.

Chances are, you may feel the same way about your current job, but you see no way to get out of it any time soon. Maybe you run your own business, but it's not the source of joy for you that you hoped it would be. But, you keep doing it anyway, because you rely on the money to pay your bills and to remain a responsible member of society.

Live like You're Retired—Right *Now*

After I've shown you how to completely redefine work, and how to put work in its proper perspective, you'll see how to easily free yourself and start living the life you hoped you might live when you retire—and start living that life *right now*.

First, I have one more task for you.

You need to create a sublist, below each job you've held, on your reordered jobs list. Each of these sublists will be made up of your favorite things *about* each job. Items on these sublists should include favorite duties and tasks you were required to perform. It can even include the types of people you got to work with as part of the job, or new things you got to learn while working. You don't have to have *liked* the job itself to find something that you liked that was a part of it.

Try to find at least one item for each job on your list.

Here's what Jenny's list looks like, after she's added her sublists:

- Third grade teacher
  - Helping the kids "get it" on any subject and seeing their eyes light up when they did
  - Hearing from parents that what the kids learned at school was affecting them positively at home
  - Knowing I'm making a real difference in people's lives
- Assistant school librarian
  - Helping kids find the perfect book
  - Knowing my job helped kids appreciate books and hopefully learn to love them for their entire lives
  - Sharing my love for books with the kids
- Clothing store clerk
  - Helping customers find the *perfect* clothing for their situation
  - Getting great discounts on the latest fashions my mother would never buy me
  - Learning how the retailing business works from the other side of the counter
- Candy striper
  - Making peoples' lives more comfortable
  - Knowing that what I'm is doing is really helping people

21

— Seeing the "inside view" of working in a hospital, even though it eventually made me queasy

- Data entry clerk

  — Gloria, Tom, and Albert—the best friends I've ever had

  — Starting out in a big company, so I was anonymous, unknown, and had no limits on making new social contacts

  — Learning and using the new technologies involved in the business

  — Being pretty much left alone to do my job my way, as long as it gets done

- Fast food salesclerk

  — Free food at a time in my life when it didn't matter what I ate

  — It got me out of the house during my teen years, when it mattered so much to me that I not be home

  — I got to meet a lot of people—customers *and* fellow employees

The secret here is that we're not looking for *jobs* you especially liked, so much as the *tasks* and *duties* that appealed most to you while you were working those jobs.

Is This Really Important?

I'm sure you've heard the old adage that if you do what you love doing most, the money will surely follow. There are plenty of extremely popular self-help books that make this point with fervor.

I heartily disagree.

You can't truly experience the exhilaration of FUN Money without being passionate about your work. This part *is* true. But, when you properly *combine* what you love doing most with the things you have the most *experience* doing, this is when the *fun* really begins.

Since we're aiming for FUN Money, you should first go through your list of interests—those things you most enjoy doing or have enjoyed doing most—and compare it against your list of job tasks that you've also enjoyed the most.

Are there any similarities? Is one of your jobs also on your list of favorite things to do? Most people rarely place a job on their favorite activities lists, but you should ask yourself if there are any jobs you've held that might belong there. Add them if you have.

And count yourself lucky. If your current job fits on your list of favorite things that you've done, you are extremely lucky—but keep reading, anyway. There is nothing wrong with having *two* FUN Money sources.

What about favorite tasks and duties on the sublists beneath any of the jobs on your jobs list? Are any of them already on your list of favorite activities? Do any belong there?

If you feel they do, add them.

I assure you—there's a method to this apparent madness. The lists you've just created (or those you will eventually create, after you've read completely through this book and you go back through to do the exercises) are the most important lists you could ever make.

They're much more important than any grocery list could be. They're more valuable than any to-do list. These are actually lists of the gold that already resides within you. This is gold you can exchange for a life of fun—the life you wish for while working right now. The life you pray one day you can afford to enjoy.

It's the start of the new life you'll soon be living.

Now—read through your favorite activities list again. This was the first list you put together. Put a star next to each item on your list that you could do all day long, that you would most likely *never* tire of doing. These will be the things you already do every chance you get—even without earning money doing them. Chances are, you even pay to do them.

There should be stars on half of the list, if not more.

If your list of favorite activities is gold—the items you just starred are pure platinum. Each starred item is a "most likely suspect" in your quest for FUN Money.

WHERE YOU ARE NOW—AND WHY

If you have a job that you love, congratulations. You're already earning FUN Money. Unless, of course, there are *other* activities that you love doing even more. As I said, there is no rule you can't have multiple sources of FUN Money.

To determine whether or not your dream job is also a great FUN Money vehicle for you, pay careful attention to your thoughts and activities through a couple of days at work. Do you find yourself thinking about other things? Are you anxious to get off the clock and head home? Do you have problems getting up in time to easily get to work on time?

Or—do you jump out of bed each day, eager to get started?

Would you do what you now do for a living, even if you weren't being paid? Would you still do it, even if you had to do something else for a living, just to pay the bills so you could continue?

These are all signs that you and your job were made for each other.

There are always at least a few people in every job who are totally happy to be doing what they do for a living. You can consider yourself extremely lucky if this is you. It might not feel like it, but you've won life's lottery.

Some police, schoolteachers, attorneys, lawn care professionals, sanitation engineers—you name it—are perfectly happy with their work, love every minute and look forward to each new day.

But, usually, they're far and away the exception to the rule.

Even if you love your current job or profession, the question still stands: would you do it every spare moment possible, even if you didn't get paid?

Or, perhaps you're absolutely head over heels in love with your current job—but it doesn't pay enough to cover the bills, let alone provide you with some fun time for doing those activities you love doing most.

Jenny would be a schoolteacher at this very moment—but schoolteachers, sadly, are of the most underpaid groups of professionals in America and throughout most of the world.

If you love your job, but never can seem to save enough to ensure a happy retirement and to pursue some of your other favorite activities, you still need to find your source of FUN Money.

FUN Money is your key to true fulfillment and happiness. Even if you love your current job or profession, even if you don't care that your current job or profession doesn't make much money. FUN Money is about having *fun* doing what you do to live *and* turning what you think is most fun into something that pays you better than most jobs would pay.

That's why, regardless of how you feel about your job today, regardless of whether or not you already own a business of your own—you still need to make those lists and work through this process with me. It could be a process of discovery for you, pointing out where you would *really* be happiest.

Even if you are one of the rare few lucky ones—include the job or profession or business you love on your list of favorite activities. Then, go through the list. Star the item or items you would be more than willing to do all day long, every day, even if you didn't earn any money doing them.

It's More Important than You Might Think

For the *rest* of us, FUN Money is even more imperative. It's essential to our well-being and to our chances for a future that's worth looking forward to living.

The vast majority of us work at whatever job or profession we can find that will best pay the bills. Paying the bills is most certainly required, if you intend to be a productive member of society.

Sadly, however, we tend to give up the bulk of our lives just to stay alive. Often, we're left with very little energy or money when it comes time to enjoy what little time is left when we're not at work—*if* there's any additional money to have some fun with and *if* there's any time in which to have it.

Even worse, most of us wind up with jobs we despise or running businesses we don't find fulfilling because of a completely wrong-headed notion about the very nature of work. This notion forces us to believe that work that's too easy or too much fun isn't *really* work at all. We actually feel better when we're working if we're *not* enjoying the work, because it feels *right*—and we've been taught all our lives that work isn't *supposed* to be fun *or* easy.

Today, thanks to the power of the Internet, you can easily start an information-based business or add information publishing to your existing business, and start a home-based business doing what you love doing most.

It's so easy, I have to laugh when I hear someone say they want to get out of their job, but they simply don't know what to do.

But—it's not really your fault that you feel this way.

You are where you are right now because you were misled from childhood. You were raised to believe that the only way to get ahead in the world is to go to school, study hard, get a degree, and work for a major corporation.

And it's not *supposed* to be fun—or it's not *really* work.

The only acceptable substitutes to this theory appear to be attorneys and doctors. It seems it's okay to dream of being a doctor with your own lucrative private practice. Just don't be so foolish as to assume you can also have fun running that private practice.

Small wonder two of the largest groups of clients that I work with on a regular basis are doctors and lawyers looking for a way to get into online businesses, so they can start *enjoying* their work.

You're Building the Perfect Dream Business

In this book, we're putting together the perfect dream business that you'll absolutely love to be a part of—one capable of completely changing your life. I guarantee, as you move forward and your life starts to change, you'll start getting a *lot* of strange advice—and even stranger quizzical looks—from your friends and family and neighbors.

That's because everyone else was misled, just like you were. They simply don't "get it." They fail to understand how anyone wandering outside in her bathrobe to pick up the morning paper at noon—just as they're pulling into the drive for a hurried lunch before speeding back to the office—could *possibly* be doing anything constructive.

They'll think all sorts of bad things. They'll assume you're breaking the law. Perhaps they'll whisper that you must have inherited a trust fund.

Let them whisper. That's part of the fun.

My mother (God love her) *still* wishes I'd just go and get a "real" job, so I can have a "secure" future, even though my business has been generating average revenues of $1 million every year for the past 23 years.

There's nothing wrong with any of these people. They might give advice that, after reading this book, no longer makes any sense—but don't blame them. Most likely, they genuinely care about you and want only the best for you, but they simply don't know any better way.

Even my mom was misled.

Most of us were led to believe that there is simply no way we could possibly have enough experience or enough money or enough time and energy to start a business of our own, let alone create valuable information products that people will eagerly buy.

But—that's exactly what you're going to be doing *very* soon. (Please—turn off your own "internal skeptic" and trust me here—it's really so very easy to do, you'll find yourself laughing out loud when we get into the nuts and bolts of it all.)

Soon, you'll be able to shake your head in pity at these well-meaning naysayers. For now, you'll just have to trust me. I have faith in you, and I know you'll be able to carry out the simple tasks required to change your life forever.

In years past, these well-meaning folks were exactly right. It wasn't that long ago that starting any business required a minimum of $10,000 cash—more often $100,000 and up. And the odds were horrifically against it working out.

Thanks to the Internet, anyone capable of navigating the World Wide Web, typing, and cutting and pasting on a computer can launch a business following my system, with little or even no money. And they can do so with a reasonable expectation that they will earn at least enough money in that business to comfortably pay for all the fun activities they love doing most. It's entirely possible to *replace* a middle-class job in the process, so fun becomes your full-time profession.

The Impossible Is Now Possible

In the past, it was impossible to focus on a tight niche, such as one of your favorite hobbies or activities, and make significant money, if you made any money at all. Before the Internet, most businesses were almost entirely focused on a single locality. The city in which you started your business had to be able to support the niche your business served, or you had to broaden your business, to appeal to more people.

If you loved working with stained glass, and you lived in a town of only 15,000 people, you were most likely out of luck. There wouldn't be enough other people interested in your niche to support a business supplying that niche.

The only alternative was to enter the risky world of mail order. This was, before the Internet explosion, the one way brave souls could expand their markets beyond a locality and reach more people with a more specialized niche interest.

Mail order is a far less expensive way to start a business than opening a brick-and-mortar store. It definitely expands the size of the market you can reach with your sales messages. Direct mail is also an extremely effective way to make sales. But it's still expensive by most standards. And the resulting risk can be tremendous.

Even a simple direct mail sales letter and order form with a return envelope can easily cost upwards of $1 to print and mail these days. Catalogs and more elaborate sales letters can cost much more. Sending that $1 letter to 10,000 people had better return at least $20,000 in orders, or you're going to start feeling pinched very quickly.

Today, thanks to the Internet, anyone with any amount of money and with very limited skills can pick an extremely focused niche and launch a business serving that niche in a way that no other business is serving it—then reach an audience of more than one billion people, all of whom are potential prospects.

I've got clients earning a great full-time living selling to just 500 or 1,000 online customers. Out of the more than one billion people currently online, I feel strongly that anyone can find a way to attract enough customers to make virtually *any* business niche work—and realize tremendous potential for profit.

Three-Step Formula for Success

Just use my simple three-step formula, and you can launch or build *any* business—home-based or brick-and-mortar, part-time or full-time:

1. Publish an e-book (an electronic book).
2. Publish an e-zine (an electronic newsletter).
3. Tie the two together and give them away for free (the easiest sale you'll ever make).

Yes—that's all there is. Only three steps. I realize that "publish a book" might sound hard. And "publish an e-zine" could seem a bit daunting, as well. Giving them both away free? It's probably a bit hard to see how that will make you any money—yet.

Keep reading. There are, admittedly, several substeps involved in each of these three main steps. I'll explain them all as we go along.

I'll even explain how you'll make great money giving all this away for free.

For now, just keep that three-step formula in mind as we move through the steps of building your FUN Money business. You can apply this three-step formula and guarantee your chances of success, because this formula works for literally *anyone*.

Yes—I said anyone, including you. You've already started by making the lists. You're already starting to move through the microsteps.

And—what we've done so far is about as tough as the work gets. You're doing fine.

The good news is that the steps *and* microsteps involved are all so simple even a 10-year-old can do them. I don't believe following these simple steps is a lot to ask in return for a complete financial and emotional makeover . . . do you?

First, Find the *Perfect* Niche

First, we have to determine the very *best* business for you to launch. To discover this, let's carefully study both of the lists you just created.

On your two lists, examine the relationships between your past work life and the fun things you truly enjoy doing. You should see that you already possess experience and knowledge—even genuine "insider" know-how—on one or more subjects.

We're going to apply that experience and knowledge to build your business on the Internet—a business that's capable of feeding eager buyers who are willing to pay a premium for whatever it is you'd like to sell. I'll even help you decide what to sell.

Looking at Jenny's lists, I can see several strong repeating themes and connections that could be capitalized on. Her love of reading and teaching stand out clearly. These skills are very valuable when it comes to running an online business. Throughout her lists, I also see a love of helping people over and over again. Even when she was working as a clerk at a clothing store, she most enjoyed helping people.

This exposure to retailing can be of some help, too, although Jenny probably doesn't realize how much information about the actual work-ings of the retail business she might have picked up while she was there.

Then there's Jenny's love of Barbie—and shopping and eBay.

The horseback riding might just have to wait a bit. She'll have plenty of time and money to enjoy all the horseback riding she wants to enjoy later—after her business is up and rolling, automated, and bringing in money round-the-clock, even while she hits the stables.

Believe it or not, there's also a way to work Jenny's love of horse-back riding in, if she really wanted to. There honestly are no limits to what you can do with your own business when you conduct business online the way I'm showing you.

Me? I wish there had been a book like this when I was starting out. I naturally gravitated toward what I truly loved doing. I hated working for someone else so much that my life was doomed if I didn't find a way to turn my fun into money—so I just jumped in with both feet and figured it out as I went along.

My early attempts at FUN Money were expensive lessons. Before computers and online communications networks started connecting the world, my FUN Money was almost always eaten up by typesetting, printing, mailing, and advertising expenses, leaving very little room for profit and adding a lot of risk to my endeavors.

Fortunately, I was a househusband and my wife at the time was a professional, bringing more money into the household than I could ever pull in working at any job I was qualified to hold. This enabled me to stay at home and raise my kids (a blessing), but it also meant I could only work at businesses that I could operate around my kids' schedules.

This news should please any stay-at-home parent reading this. Yes, my system will work for you, too. Your situation is perfect for bringing in FUN Money.

I knew the formula, but the vehicle that made it a nonstop never-fail formula didn't appear until the advent of the early dial-up computer bulletin boards (BBSs) that predated the World Wide Web by more than 10 years.

That's when I took off like wildfire, writing and publishing online, following my passions, and often generating more money in some single months than I ever imagined I would make in a lifetime.

Even though I had the benefit of my love of reading, writing, and publishing going for me, it took years for me to finally put them together, before the FUN Money could begin.

You have this book—the benefit of my 23+ years of FUN Money experience to guide you. During all this time, I've also discovered a multitude of ways to easily apply the FUN Money principles I'm teaching here, to launch a successful business without spending *any* money, part-time or full-time—and without writing a word, if you don't want to.

I think I said this before. At the risk of repeating myself: Lucky you.

You can choose to sell physical or digital products. You can provide consulting services. You can even bring people together, broker deals, and take a slice of *their* combined profits.

How you ultimately apply the principles taught in this book is entirely up to you.

There is an endless amount of money to be made on the Internet today. And the pot of gold at the end of the Internet rainbow only continues to grow exponentially. Don't think for a minute that you don't have the skills or knowledge to pull it off, either. You've already taken the first steps. You should already know of at least *one* niche interest area where you have some experience and knowledge that other people would pay to access.

Put both of the lists that you just made in a safe place. We'll return to them again.

GETTING WHERE YOU WANT TO BE—*FAST*

I said this is easy and it really is. Let's take a closer look at each of the three steps in my system, and you'll see what I mean:

1. Publish an e-book.

2. Publish an e-zine.

3. Tie them both together and give 'em away for free.

Notice, in these three steps, I said "publish" an e-book (a digital book), not "write" an e-book. Writing *any* book can be difficult and time consuming. Even if writing a book is something you'd *love* doing, you could spend several months struggling with this task. FUN Money is *not* about struggle.

Don't even *think* about writing an e-book yourself.

Don't worry. I'll show you some ways that you can quickly put together an e-book that people will value in three or four days—one week tops.

The same goes for an e-zine. Writing a newsletter is not only difficult and time consuming—it's a routine that you have to keep up, week after week or month after month, on deadline.

I'll be showing you ways to easily put together a *great* electronic newsletter people will anticipate and look forward to reading each time you release a new issue.

Again, I'm going to show you how to publish this e-zine without writing a word, unless you're just dying to spend some of your time putting your own words on paper. (I'm not out to *stifle* creativity here—but I do want you to see that there is *no* creative "talent" required for my system to work.)

Actually, the hardest part of the process is simply deciding what you're going to focus on, so you know you're setting up your system to create real sales from your efforts. Implementing the system itself is so easy you'll probably find there are ways you can do it in your sleep.

Getting Started: Some Easy Research

And—it all starts with some of the easiest research you'll ever do. Those lists I had you start working on are the first phase of research you needed to do, to discover your true passion and your areas of expertise. And to see where they might intersect.

If you didn't create your two lists, you might want to do that now. It's up to you—but it really will make the rest of this process a *lot* easier for you if you follow along and start getting things set up now.

Do this, and you could easily launch your system shortly after finishing this book.

Back to the lists.

You now have two lists. Study both of them. Hopefully, you'll map out some direct connections between your favorite activities and interests and your personal experiences and skills. In Jenny's case, it was obvious the first time I talked to her that her first choice should be something related to collecting Barbie dolls.

Soon, we'll put her system together. I'm betting, because of the lists I know she's put together, that she heads in the direction of Barbie collecting. Her love of Barbie is too prevalent to ignore.

But—it goes deeper than that.

Jenny not only loves collecting Barbies—she reveres them. She loves nothing more than fussing with them; researching their history; and buying, selling, and trading them. And she's never let her fascination with them falter since she was first introduced to Barbie at a very early age.

It's a natural for her. She's been collecting Barbies, devoting so much time to her passion that, to almost any other Barbie collector, she's an *expert*. And she doesn't even realize it. Yet.

All we'll need to do is focus on that interest and *establish* Jenny as an expert, then she'll be off and running.

Of course, I'll show you the process, too.

Is there anything on your lists that fits this pattern? You want to look for activities you've already devoted a lot of time and energy to. If they're things that you already know a great deal about, these activities and interests are worth investigating deeper.

This is, most likely, the one you should go after.

You *Are* an Expert

You're going to use my system to establish yourself as an expert in your niche interest. Believe it or not, you are an expert if you've been doing anything longer than a month. After that, there's always someone just getting started who could learn from you.

Of course—the longer you've been doing something, the more you presumably know about it. This broadens your market. But— seriously—I've seen clients take up a brand new hobby, learn all they can about it for a month, then turn around and start making money helping other people who are just getting started in that same hobby.

Even better, when we look at Jenny's lists, there are a number of *other* complimentary skills—activities and tasks that she not only enjoys doing, but that she also has invested some considerable time doing.

These skills—some of the other items on her list—will come in extremely handy as I work with her to build a profitable Barbie-based business.

Can you imagine the reaction Jenny's in for when she tells her mother she's planning to start a full-time Barbie business? I'm pretty sure she'll be in for some serious ribbing from Tom, Gloria, and Andy, too.

Your lists might differ quite a bit from Jenny's. The lists Tom, Gloria, and Albert will put together later don't match Jenny's, either.

Find the Money

Because it's tough to have fun when you have no money, the first step to FUN Money is discovering which of your number one favorite activities you can turn into a *profitable* business. You don't want to be a starving artist. The arts are a blast. Who hasn't watched their favorite musician and dreamed of the life he or she must lead? The good news is, if you love painting, drawing, writing, or music, for example, you're already in perhaps the best position possible from which to launch a Fun Money business.

But, I've found that hunger can get in the way of even the biggest fun you could imagine—every time.

You *must* turn what you love doing most into money.

What you're learning right here will enable you to turn whatever artistic endeavor you ever wanted to pursue into cash. Remember, though—it doesn't matter how good or bad you are. It doesn't even matter if you can't write or paint or take pictures or play music. It's easy to launch a profitable online business around your favorite pastime, whether you can write or paint or sing anything.

You can find out everything you need to know with some simple Internet research.

This is easy to do. You can do it in your spare time, at home, or wherever you have access to a computer and an Internet connection. It only takes a short time to determine which of your passions is potentially most profitable, so it's definitely worth the small effort required.

Niches within Niches within Niches

In the process, you'll also determine the perfect niche area within your passion (something I call the "niche within a niche"). This is your "sweet spot" for maximum online sales and profits. The Internet is ripe with subniches that you can dominate quickly, for maximum results.

If you plan to start any business on the Internet, it's always best to first check out how many search engine pages relate directly to your passion. Then, you want to look at the number of people who are actually typing keywords and phrases that relate to the niche business you hope to start into the search engines, to find information and products they want.

A quick visit to Google shows that there are more than 2,240,000 pages online, indexed by Google, related to the search term "Barbie collector." 2,660,000 pages show up when you enter "Barbie information." "Rare Barbie dolls" brings up 1,130,000 pages. There are 1,410,000 online pages referencing "Barbie doll club" and 2,360,000 pages referencing "Barbie doll clothes."

It's interesting to note this simple search for "Barbie clothes" turned up as many related pages as our search for "Barbie collectors."

34

Wow. That's what I call a fat, potentially profitable niche within a niche.

We'll look deeper into these web pages in a moment. Next, we want to visit one of Google's competitors in the search engine world—Yahoo—and take a look at the number of people who are actually typing keywords and phrases related to Barbie into the search engines.

About Those Keywords and Phrases

First, in case you're not familiar with the term, *keywords* are the *exact* words and phrases people type into a search engine when they're seeking either free information or products and services to buy on the Web.

Whether you knew it or not, you were using keywords every time you looked for web sites using a search engine. Keywords are those words or phrases that you type into the "search bar" on a search engine, to find what you're looking for.

This might be basic information for some of you. Too bad. A lot of people still don't know what a keyword is, and this is essential to setting up a profitable FUN Money business, so bear with us.

Yahoo has a service that's a lot like Google's Adwords program. Adwords is the driving force behind Google's enormous financial success. It's the place where companies and individuals doing business on the Web can place ads on Google that will then display in the search engine's web site lists, as "sponsored listings." They normally appear to the *right* of the search engine-generated list of sites that comes up when you enter selected keywords. We refer to this as the "organic" listing.

Sometimes these sponsored links also appear *above* the free listings in addition to the list that appears to the right.

You buy Adwords ads on Google by bidding on them. First, you write a small ad (smaller than most classified ads) that you want to have displayed on Google, following Google's guidelines for creating sponsored listing ads. You then apply as many different related keywords and keyword combinations as you can come up with to each ad that you create. Your ad will then appear in the "sponsored links" area whenever someone types in the keywords or combinations you selected for your "campaign."

Advertisers choose the amount of money they're willing to pay Google for each time someone clicks on the ad they've entered into their campaigns. The higher you bid, the closer to the top of the sponsored links listings your ad will appear. It all depends on the number of other people bidding for the same keywords and how much they're willing to pay.

Sponsored links on Yahoo work pretty much the same as they do on Google. But, Yahoo offers a free tool that you can use, to see which keywords are being searched and how many people typed them into the search engine during the past month. The tool also shows you *other* keywords that might be related to the keyword you're researching, plus the number of times these alternate keywords have been typed into Yahoo in the past month.

This is extremely useful free information.

You can access this free tool at: http://inventory.overture.com.

On Overture, we find that, in the past month, as of this writing, "Barbie doll collector" was entered into Yahoo Search 1,146 times.

This is a good number. More than 1,000 people typed "Barbie doll collector" into the Yahoo search engine in the past month. I'd be happier if there were more but, as long as it's not *less* than 1,000, it's worth noting this keyword phrase.

Because this number is a little small, you also want to back it out a bit and search on a more general keyword. Let's try "Barbie doll."

This brings up the following list:

44,869	Barbie doll
4,923	Barbie doll house
4,336	Dress-up Barbie doll game
1,916	Collectible Barbie doll
1,730	Barbie doll picture
1,539	Vintage Barbie doll
1,146	Barbie doll collector
977	Barbie doll clothes

Notice that "Barbie doll clothes" has less than 1,000 searches, but I included it anyway. It's close—and there were so many other search terms related to Barbie dolls with less searches, I fudged a little.

This Is a Science That Can Be Duplicated

This is a science that can be duplicated—but there's a bit of art involved, too. In the end, you'll be good going with what feels best, but this simple research will assist you in focusing.

From this first list, I can see a *perfect*, strong subniche for Jenny, in addition to Barbie doll clothes. Can you guess which one?

Notice that "collectible Barbie doll," "Barbie doll collector" and "vintage Barbie doll" are searched more often than "Barbie doll clothes." These three point directly to a subniche that deserves careful consideration.

I have *no idea* why "dress-up Barbie doll game" has more than 4,000 searches a month. This is the kind of thing that can crop up during this part of the process, and it can easily point you to possible profitable niches that you might never have thought of without this research.

That's why this research is so important. It's absolutely the *least* fun you're going to have with this entire process—but it's vital to getting the process started, so you don't unwittingly walk into a "profit-free zone."

If every artist in the world would follow this process before they created anything, there would no longer be such a thing as a starving artist.

Before we wrap up our research, let's also check out the other search terms we entered into Google:

Barbie Collector
- 3,823 searches for "Barbie collector"
- 1,146 searches for "Barbie doll collector"

This is good stuff. There is definitely a market for Jenny's expertise here.

Barbie Information
- 34 searches for "Barbie general hisory information vintage" (notice the misspelling of "history")
- 30 information barrie (*another* misspelling—both of these are pretty much worthless, however)

Rare Barbie Dolls
- Nothing

Barbie Doll Club
- Nothing

I'm baffled by the total lack of searches for "Rare Barbie dolls" and "Barbie doll club," when there are so many searches for "Barbie doll collector" and "Barbie collector."

Usually, this is where your own intimate knowledge of your chosen niche will prove to be one of your most valuable assets in this process. I'm not a Barbie doll fanatic. I don't have *any* intimate knowledge of the market for information, products, and services of interest to other Barbie fanatics.

Jenny holds this piece of the puzzle. I'll have to tap her for that later. You hold this key to your own FUN Money path as well.

For now, get started. Make a list of keywords. Play with Overture's free keyword lookup tool. See how many related phrases and words you can find . . . track them for traffic and start the comparison process, so you can identify your true path.

I said this is the hardest part of the entire process. It's only difficult at all because *some* of it relies on instinct. You have to examine your two lists, create keywords for *all* of the possible niches and niches within niches you discover in your research, see how many people are looking for the terms you've discovered—and make a determination as to the viability of any given niche or subniche you wish to pursue.

The good news is that the "gut" reaction portion of this process is almost completely *your* gut—based on your intimate knowledge of the niche or subniche you've decided to go after as you continue to dig your own FUN Money mine.

You don't want to rush this part of the process. But, don't allow paralysis by analysis freeze you up, either. It's possible to switch your niche after you've chosen one—if it doesn't work out. I want you to get through this process quickly and painlessly—so you can move on to the FUN Money *fast*.

FUN MONEY PROFILE

Erik D. Stafford

Stafford Marketing, LLC.
www.thefasterwebmaster.com
www.fwmsilversessions.com

Previous jobs held: Restaurant waiter, bartender, retail store manager, delicatessen manager, landscaper, designer, web designer, creative director, marketing director.

Least favorite thing about working for someone else: Being tied to a set schedule and a set dress code, being a slave to the paycheck, and also not being able to make larger-scale decisions regarding positioning, packaging, marketing, hiring, promotion, and sales.

Favorite thing about working for someone else: The interaction with other coworkers, the sense of camaraderie.

Single pivotal moment or thing that helped make the switch to pursuing a FUN Money lifestyle: I've always been an entrepreneur. I only usually took a "real" job when I felt pressure to do so. In high school, I sold airbrushed jackets for money. In college, I sold paintings. I sold my paintings for several years and had several shows. I've worked for myself, as a webmaster or design contractor—mostly from home—on and off since 2000.

In 2002, my wife and daughter and I moved to the Caribbean. It had always been our dream to live in the islands . . . and we did it. For almost three years, we lived the slow life under the sun. Category 5 hurricane Ivan hit the Cayman Islands on the 11th of September, 2004. Our condo was gone. The jobs, the cars, all of our belongings . . . all of it was gone. We ended up in Miami, homeless, feeling very lucky to be alive, and very disappointed to have our island lifestyle come to an end.

Believe it or not, though, it was the best thing that ever happened to me. I ended up meeting a few people in my personal life who introduced me to Internet marketing, which has changed my life dramatically. I got back on my feet. I learned the industry. I launched my first project, and I met some amazingly talented people.

Emotional reactions when making the decision to quit the day job: As you get older and have kids and mounting responsibilities and a bigger monthly "nut" to make, it becomes much harder to take chances on new businesses and moves to other countries. It's always accompanied by fear, worry, excitement, "can I really do this?" and so on, and so on. I'm lucky to have a very supportive wife.

Reaction of your friends, family, and loved ones to your decision:
Most of it was, "Here goes Erik with another one of his cockeyed
schemes again" type stuff. I've been involved in (and walked away
from) several failed businesses and partnerships.

Time required to attain the FUN Money lifestyle: Six months . . . if
that. I'd been reading a lot about the laws of attraction, and I knew
what I was doing would work.

What you do now: I work from my home in southwest Florida. I
spend my days on the phone or writing e-mail. I do a lot of Internet
marketing, product development, and promotion. I work when I want.
I find that, despite all these freedoms, I actually work just as hard as I
ever did . . . probably because I enjoy it so much.

Your life today: We are enjoying life, that's for sure. I have two kids
under the age of five, and it's a pleasure to spend more time with
them. It's summer here in Florida, as I write this, and we're taking a
lot of time off. We're swimming a lot. Next summer, we're going back
to the Caribbean—to the Cayman Islands, where we used to live—for
a month.

Advice for other FUN Money seekers: Don't give up when everyone doubts you. Just take that doubt and turn it into motivation.

Wrap-Up

- Change your attitude about work.
- Make a list of at least 10 things you've loved doing most and
  could do all day, given the opportunity.
- Reorder your list, arranging the things you've done the most at
  the top.
- Next, make a list of jobs you've held in your life. Every job
  you've held, good or bad.
- Reorder list number two, putting the job you liked most at the
  top, and working down the list.

- Below each item on your reordered list, build a sublist of the things you most liked about each job—at least one item per job on the list.
- Compare your list of things you love doing most with the list of job experiences you enjoyed.
- Look for past jobs you've held that you can add to your list of favorite things. It's rare—but it happens.
- If your current job fits on your list of favorite things—keep going. There is nothing wrong with having *two* FUN Money sources.
- Star the items on your favorite activities list that you could do all day every day.
- Look for connections between your favorite activities and the work you've done.
- Any interest that meets the other criteria and has connections to your work is strengthened by that connection, providing background experience and knowledge.
- Look on Google.com for search words related to your interest.
- Visit http://inventory.overture.com and test keywords related to your chosen niche.
- Drill down to the perfect niche within a niche.

CHAPTER 2

WHICH FRIEND ARE *YOU*?

I think of life itself now as a wonderful play that I've written for myself, and so my purpose is to have the utmost fun playing my part.

—Shirley MacLaine

When Jenny first saw a DVD of one of my live presentations, she was floored. She'd always felt there was more she could be doing to better her own life. And she knew her teaching abilities were being wasted.

When she heard the presentation I gave about the power of self-publishing on the Internet to create unique information products easily, she was immediately excited. What I taught on that DVD opened her mind to possibilities she'd never before imagined.

Here was a talented person with a genuine passion and knowledge that other people would benefit from—and she's an experienced teacher, too. Still, she spends the bulk of her waking hours working in a cubicle, entering data and running spreadsheets for a large company that doesn't really appreciate her.

She comes in and does the work that is expected of her. And she does it well. But whenever she gets a chance, she browses the Web looking at Barbies, researching, and dreaming—counting the minutes until she can finally clock out and go home to start having some *real* fun.

At home, she rushes through her routine—cooking and cleaning, grocery shopping, and doing a bit of laundry—so she can spend the last remaining two or three hours of the day spending time with her friends and family. . . and working on her doll collection.

It's as if her entire life (at least, the portion of her life that really mattered to her) was condensed into those few evening and weekend hours. Ten hours of almost every day, (including the hour it takes her to get to work and back) aren't hers. They belong to her boss. To the company that pays her. She's trading in the majority of her waking life for the ability to stay alive, hoping for a little time left over, to do what she loves doing most.

Does this sound like you? Don't you feel this way at least *some* of the time?

Even people who already own their own businesses often don't realize they've merely switched one job for another. They followed their dream of starting a business to live more like they always wanted to, only to find that the business can own them, too. And it can own them for many more hours every day than any regular job will.

If you're frustrated a little, that's okay. It's a sign you're waking out of the trance and starting to see your life for what it really is. This is the first step toward turning your life into the FUN Money life you deserve—and it's the most painful step you'll take.

JENNY GETS STARTED

Jenny's a reasonably happy, well-balanced person or her situation might have nearly driven her insane by now.

When she saw that DVD presentation where I discussed my three-step FUN Money system, she called my office at the first opportunity.

"I don't know what happened," she told me. As I was watching your presentation on that DVD, I realized how unhappy I've been. It was the first time I've ever clearly seen how much time I've wasted not getting started before now—and how easy it is to turn it around and get a business going that frees me to spend more time doing what I love doing most.

"The clincher was the way you seem to be having so much fun doing what you're doing."

"Thanks," I replied. "I'm devoted to having more fun every day."

That's how I started working with Jenny.

She told me about her past and what she's been doing, her interests, and what she does for a living today. I knew I could help her. I've never seen anyone who follows and applies the steps I'm laying out for you in this book fail. Period.

I set up a series of appointments with Jenny, and we started rolling through the research steps I've already revealed. I was relieved when Jenny decided she would be happiest doing something to serve Barbie collectors.

I'd already identified Barbie as Jenny's true passion before she realized it was.

Many times, we downplay those things we love doing most, never considering them as an option when we seek out a way to earn a living—simply because the things we love doing most don't *feel* like work.

Today, the Internet gives all of us the ability to easily launch part-time businesses from a kitchen table, compete with major corporations, and grow those businesses into something that more than replaces the income we used to make working for someone else.

Because the Internet is so vast and reaches so many people, you can focus on what I call "micro-niches," or niches within niches. These are areas of interest to people *within* a group of people interested in similar things.

Rather than pets, you can focus, for example, on iguanas. Rather than dachsunds, you can focus on designer collars for dachsunds.

This is why it's so important that you first go through the steps I detailed in Chapter 1, to identify your real interests and strengths, then tie them to a subniche within your own niche interest. The Internet is like one giant community with a population of more than *one billion* citizens. It's surprisingly easy, on the Internet, to launch a business serving extremely specific subniches and still find hundreds or even thousands of people who are interested in what you might have to sell.

And with virtually *no* serious competition for the system you're now putting together.

Just make sure the subniche you've chosen, within the subject you're most passionate about, is one that other people are interested in. Then make sure people are spending money on this subniche. Then you can easily start a business serving that subniche, without risking your life savings in the process.

Here's a fun way to see if people spend money on your subniche. Go do it. Participate in your passion and notice how much money you spend. Are there people you can buy things from? How many? Are there any magazines supporting your subniche—or some subniche advertisers within publications serving the larger niche?

These are all signs of profitable subniches.

I hear you thinking, "If it's that easy, why isn't everyone doing it?" I understand your skepticism. This is the same kind of skepticism you'll be dealing with regularly after beginning your journey with me—from everyone around you.

This sort of thinking is a direct result of that well-meaning upbringing we received from from people who were also raised to believe that work isn't *supposed* to be fun *or* easy (let alone both) and, therefore, anything truly fun that you might attempt to do to make a living is suspect.

This kind of thinking is easy to explain.

A DIFFERENT DEFINITION OF WORK

As we moved into the Information Age, our notion of work changed from one based on trading physical labor for money to trading our *mental* labor or capabilities for money. Today, our jobs are just as likely to consist of talking on the phone, typing, attending meetings, or pushing buttons, as they are to have anything to do with performing physical labor.

This shift mars our mental picture of work as we were taught it's *supposed* to be. If we're not physically *working* to earn a living any more, then we must change our definition of work. One way to change our mental image of work and still keep that new image in line with what we were raised to believe is to hold onto the belief that, while the work we do for a living isn't necessarily physically *hard* any more, it still can't be *fun*—or it isn't work.

This makes it easier to justify working jobs we don't care for, trading our knowledge and our time for dollars instead of our physical labor.

If you don't believe this, try a little experiment. Go to someone you know who cares for you a lot—a parent, a spouse, a sibling, or a good friend. Proudly announce you're going to quit your job to pursue your passion, which you've decided is—. (Insert whatever niche interest you decided on from Chapter 1 here.)

Check out the reaction. I'll bet it ranges anywhere from gasping disbelief to worry to open admonitions to "come to your senses" and "straighten up."

It doesn't matter if you plan to work hard around-the-clock pursuing your dream. It doesn't matter what skills you might have to make it happen—or who you know or what help you might have lined up to get you to success. Very few people who really care about you will ever tell you to drop everything and "go for it."

I'm not going to tell you to give up your day job yet. You don't have to risk your life savings, quit your job, or give up anything but an hour or two a day to start a business on the Internet, the way I'm going to show you. I just want you to see what reaction you will get when you say you're planning to do this because it will show you how widespread the well-meaning lie has become.

It's literally ingrained in our souls, so it takes a little work to pull it out, examine it, and see the lie for what it is—a myth. Something that worked well for society as a whole at one time, but which is now totally without merit, outdated, and useless.

Hold onto this lie, and you'll hold yourself back. . . for life.

Seek the Natural Selection

After Jenny came to the realization that her life *could* change and she knew where to find the tools to make it happen—she made a beeline toward Barbie because she understood that anything else wouldn't hold her interest. She also realized, after talking with me, that she's become quite an expert on Barbie throughout the years. And she was eager to put her teaching skills back into use, doing something that might eventually pay her better than teaching grade school did.

Jenny was enlightened and ready for the next step. She had uncovered the lie for what it was and rejected it. Have you?

Jenny's research showed that there were already some people selling to Barbie collectors on the Web. Buying and selling collectible Barbies was a passion with her—but she also liked to sew. Her research showed there were almost as many people seeking Barbie clothes on the Web as there were people looking for Barbie dolls.

There are actually more people competing in this arena—but more buyers to compete for. And the competitors appear to be smaller companies and individuals.

No Competition = No Business

"This has me worried," Jenny said. "I wanted to find a niche with no competition."

"That's almost impossible," I explained. "Most of the niches and subniches with *no* competitors are also niches and subniches with no *buyers*. Competitors are good. You want competitors because they show you where the money is. If there were no competitors in Barbie collecting or clothes, I'd tell you to look elsewhere. Even if you discovered a great niche with no competitors—the situation wouldn't stay that way for long. Eventually, someone would come along and enter your niche with you—particularly after they saw you making money."

"Most of the time, the presence of competitors actually *reduces* your risk when entering a chosen subniche. Competitors also give you successful models to study and improve on, so you don't have to reinvent the wheel."

Jenny wasn't fully reassured. "But—these people already have customers and they're established. That doesn't sound good to me."

"It's easy," I told her. "Become a customer of your competitors. Study their web sites and buy something from them. Then, study the entire process they utilized to get you to the point of purchase."

I could tell by her voice that it wasn't completely clear yet, until I went on to explain that, thanks to the World Wide Web, it's also easier than ever to spy on your competitors and beat them at their own game.

"Look at what they're doing to attract customers," I told her. "See what they provide for free on their sites. Ask yourself—can you offer more? Study the layout of their site. Can you make it easier to find just what people are looking for? Then look at the products they sell. Can you offer something even more specialized? Perhaps you can offer more choices than they do.

"When you buy something from them—do they ship it as quickly as you could? Do they provide only e-mail customer support or is there a telephone number to call? Either way, try asking a question and see if you could provide better support than they can."

"Even better," I told her, "this is shopping with a purpose. And, once you launch your business, talk to an accountant. Any shopping of this kind from now on should be tax-deductible."

Now that she saw where I was going, Jenny started nodding enthusiastically. "I get it. I can be one of their customers, then design my own business to provide what they don't."

"Exactly," I said. "This would be very hard to do in the brick-and-mortar world, without physical espionage forcing you to risk getting thrown out of stores. But, these people have no idea you're spying, planning to dive into the same niche they're currently serving. They won't know what hit them."

As I just explained to Jenny—your next step, after you've identified all the subniches within the niche you most love, is to identify the competitors already occupying that niche, then do some judicious spying. This will enable you to create a different experience for your customers, one that's unique and not currently being offered. This will be one of your most powerful keys to mapping your way to success.

Just avoid the temptation to think about lower prices as a competitive advantage. If you can offer lower prices—great. But, lower prices alone do not attract customers. The system you're now building will enable you to charge more than your competitors and still dominate your chosen subniche.

Turnabout's Fair Play

Jenny was excited now. Still, she had her doubts. "But—won't someone eventually do that to *me*?"

"Absolutely," I said. "Expect it. Embrace it. Stop thinking small. Remember you're dealing with a community of more than one *billion* people, and there is plenty of room for a lot of players at all levels. Also realize there are millions more people still moving into this Internet community every year."

"Competitors keep you on your toes and make running an Internet business more fun."

"Okay," Jenny said, a trace of disbelief still making her sound a bit unsure.

"Besides," I went on, "Your next step is going to make you stand out in ways that no competitor can ever overshadow."

"Oh?"

I had her interest now. Good. I hope I've captivated your interest, too.

I told her that, in our next session together, we would build an identity for her business that is hers and hers alone. Hands down. Solid. Built in such a way that she'll literally construct an impenetrable *wall* around every customer she acquires, so no competitor can ever touch her again.

Then, I wrapped up our session with a homework assignment. I told her to make a list of her favorite television shows. In each show, I also told her to look for the one character she most closely related to.

Jenny said she was still a bit confused—so I assume you might be, too.

After you've identified your subniche and the competitors you'll be facing, studied those competitors and started mapping out the ways you're going to differentiate your business, it's time for some *real* fun. This list will help us build the foundation of this tool.

Have some fun. Make a list of television shows you've always enjoyed. Sitcom or not. This isn't actually an integral part of my three-step system—but it's still required reading. Branding your business from the start will prove indispensable as you grow your business. I believe it will make your business grow much faster—and it could help it reach unimagined heights of success.

Don't skip branding steps simply because they're not actually a part of my three-step formula. We'll be using some simple and fun branding techniques to create a powerful weapon you can use to launch and grow your business—and it's best if you start putting this together as you prepare to launch your business for surefire results right away.

RACHEL, MONICA, CHANDLER, OR ROSS?

The next time Jenny and I got together on the phone, she was moving forward nicely. She'd identified her niche. And she'd started researching her competitors, signing up on their sites, and ordering some of their Barbie clothes and accessories.

She admitted she was already having some fun.

Jenny told me she already had some ideas for ways she could improve on what she'd seen—but she was waiting until she received the orders she'd placed before putting it all into her final plan.

We'll get to the process, later, where she puts what she's learned about her competitors into action. First—we need to build that branding tool. We'll put up an impenetrable wall your competitors can never break through and have some fun doing it.

When I asked Jenny what her all-time favorite TV show was, she replied, "*Friends*. Without a doubt, that's one of the funniest shows I've ever seen. I doubt there will ever be another comedy as good as *Friends*."

"Good choice," I replied. "I agree it was a great show, and it's *perfect* for this next exercise. One of the things that makes *any* TV show great is the characters, and *Friends* had a cast of characters that drove every story, every plot. Find *your* character in *Friends*—the one person in the story you personally resonated with the most."

I could almost hear Jenny's brows furrowing over the phone. "But—I liked them *all*—that's why it's my all-time favorite show."

"That's fine, Jenny," I said. "But—if you had to *be* one of the characters on *Friends*, which one would you most like to be? This should be the character who most fits your own character, the person you already are. The one person you would feel most comfortable being, if a genie suddenly popped out of a bottle on your desk and your wish was that you could be popped into the show."

"Ahh," she said. "That would have to be Monica. I'm pretty organized. I approach things logically. I'm extremely detail-oriented. And I'm pretty smart—I graduated college and got my teaching certificate, after all."

She paused for a moment. "And—I know I'm not cut out to be a keyboard puncher the rest of my life, that's for sure."

The Caricature Within

"Okay," I said. "Now we need to assimilate those characteristics and create a brandable persona for your business. How could we incorporate your passion for detail into your desire to teach—then fold both of those into a Barbie clothing business?"

Silence. I could hear Jenny breathing. That was all. It was apparent she was waiting for me to take the lead . . . so I did.

"What if we play up the fact that you're a teacher—maybe even create a teacher character to represent your business? She's holding a ruler in one hand and a Barbie doll in the other, looking stern with a noticeable twinkle in her eye that telegraphs the fact that she's kidding."

"Okay..."

I went on to suggest that we make her character a sewing teacher, give her a memorable name, then build Jenny's company around that.

It was getting near time for our second session to end. "Oh..." I added. "And let's make sure this teacher character looks like you."

"How do I do that," Jenny asked?

"Easy. Is there a place anywhere near you where you can hire a caricature artist?"

"What's a caricature artist?"

"It's someone who paints portraits that accent and highlight one or more of your physical attributes—so it looks kind of like a cartoon."

"Oh." she replied. "Yes. There's one down the street a few miles, closer to downtown. He sets up a canvas on the corner for a few hours every weekend and does paintings for passersby. I always called them cartoons."

"Your homework assignment, before our next meeting, is to go to the caricature artist and have him paint your portrait as a teacher, holding an over sized ruler in one hand and a Barbie doll in the other. Bring one of your favorite Barbies with you, so he can capture her as well. Ask him to make sure the Barbie you're holding is also a caricature."

WHAT ABOUT PHOEBE—OR JOEY?

You should complete the assignment I gave Jenny. Make a list of *your* favorite TV shows. Go on—this is easy stuff.

They don't all have to be sitcoms—but that's where a lot of our most loveable characters come from. There's *All in the Family, Mary Tyler Moore, Seinfeld*—and tons more shows to pick from, jam-packed with unforgettable characters.

List them.

Good dramas are also loaded with excellent characters. Look at *Rockford Files*, for example. Jim Rockford's dad, Joseph, was always getting into trouble. Jim was a great character, too—but what about that Angel guy? What a *mess*.

List just those TV shows you've really loved the most. Remember that your goal is to find a character that you resonate with, that you could most easily step into the show and play without prior rehearsal, if you had to. The character you pick should also be one who a *lot* of other people have seen or would be familiar with.

Most everyone knows who Dick Van Dyke is. Not so many people know who the third-place runner-up on the second season of *The Apprentice* is.

Combine your own most memorable characteristics with a TV show character that a lot of other people have been exposed to, that you also relate to, and you can easily create a business persona and make that persona resonate with a *lot* more people. They might never recognize any similarity between your character and the one you've modeled her after from your favorite show—but they'll instantly feel good about your company without necessarily knowing why.

Creating this character and building a business persona around him is a powerful way to differentiate your business from any competitors who currently exist or who may come up behind you and try to invade your market space.

The idea here is to build a character that *represents* you in your business environment. This makes it almost alarmingly easy to create clever catch phrases and slogans that build that character. It also makes creating promotional materials to capitalize on the character a snap.

The result? You'll become *impenetrable*. No competitor will be able to touch you because your business is *you*. Because there is only one "you" in the universe, you'll create a preferred market for other people who resonate with your persona.

No one else can ever fill those shoes.

DISCOVERING THE CHARACTER YOU REALLY PLAY IN YOUR LIFE

This is where we apply the cement to that brick wall we're building around your customers so they never again wander away to a competitor. It's the other half of the equation we started building by locating your favorite television character.

You might wind up with a copyright infringement suit if you launch a business based around Ted Knight from the *Mary Tyler Moore Show*. If, however, I blend in my hippy past, the fact that I've always been a writer and publisher, the fact that my favorite music is the blues and my favorite movies are intellectual comedies, all mixed in with Ted's traits—the silly self-absorbed weather man—I get something completely new and unique. But also still identifiable.

Develop a Profitable Persona

What we did in the last section was like pouring a big cup of coffee. Now we're going to stir in some cream and sugar.

This is where you need to get into the *real* you and discover the key elements of your core personality that most resonate with others. It's where Jenny hit a couple of snags she wasn't counting on.

To get started, you should create a survey and give it to two or three people who you know well. It's even more important that they know you very well. It's a short, simple survey most people who really love you will enjoy completing.

The purpose of this survey is to find out how you're really perceived by the people who *like* you.

Do not—repeat—*do not* give this survey to people who don't know you well and especially not to anyone who doesn't really like you. They'll have way too much fun slamming you, and you won't get any useful information from the process.

Here's what you want to know:

- What one physical feature of mine do you find most attractive?
- What emotional characteristic do you like most about me?
- What spiritual characteristic do you like most about me?
- What one thing (physical, emotional, or spiritual) do you wish I'd change?
- Describe me in three words or less.
- What TV character do I remind you of the most?

That's it. Short and sweet. If you can't find two or three people in your life willing to give you honest, caring answers to these six questions, you might want to reexamine your life and make some changes.

I'm sorry, but helping you with that problem would go beyond the scope of this book.

Jenny had Gloria, Albert, and Tom fill out her survey. That's when she hit that snag I told you about earlier. It's not what you might think. It had nothing to do with their answers.

Their answers were all over the place. I can't even tell you what physical characteristic of Jenny's Tom said he was most attracted to, but I'm reasonably certain you can guess. Gloria envied her ankles. Go figure. Albert was fascinated by her hair.

This is why I told you to ask two or *three* close friends. Five would be better but, in today's cubicle-and-online-dominated world, it's harder and harder to find people who have five *close* friends or family members. If you do have more people you can give the survey to, do so.

You need to get this simple input from as many people as you can because you want to *average* the answers and look for *patterns* in them.

This is where you'll find the *real* answers . . . the answers you need.

The answers Jenny got were helpful. She found that her hair, being naturally strawberry red and framing a happy, freckled face, was more attractive than she ever realized. And her eyes, looking large and knowing, are her friends' two favorite physical traits.

She also found that all three like her cheerful spirit and feel she is the most empathetic person in her group. Tom and Gloria wish she would spend more time with them and Albert wishes she would get more computer-savvy, so they could talk more.

The problem I mentioned? After the questionnaire, Tom, Gloria, and Albert started asking Jenny some pointed questions about what she's up to. It's a natural question to ask. After all—can you remember the last time one of your best friends handed you a survey about her and asked you to fill out your answers? It's enough to get *anyone* asking a few questions.

And Jenny, never having been the kind of person who holds anything back, told them about her discussions with me and her plans to start a business for Barbie collectors.

All three immediately wanted to change a couple of their answers to the survey. They obviously thought Jenny was crazy until she assured them that she's not quitting her job or anything right away—she's just going to start a small online business in her spare time and see where it goes.

Then they wanted to know more about me.

REINVENTING THE CHARACTER YOU *REALLY* PLAY IN YOUR LIFE

You also need to dig into your inner being a bit. Compare your own feelings about yourself and your own intimate knowledge of your past experience and feelings with those that you see on the survey you had your friends fill out.

The point is to identify your *caricature-istics* (*not* your characteristics). Caricature-istics are those traits that are most immediately memorable about you and that will immediately resonate with the most people.

It's like the caricature you had drawn of yourself—or the one you will have drawn—in writing.

Next, you want to boil all this down to two or three characteristics that will most likely resonate with the largest number of your prospective customers. Then blow them *up*, exaggerating them out of proportion. *Accent* those characteristics just like a caricature artist makes an oversized nose gigantic, and smallish ears tiny specks.

It doesn't hurt to be a bit outrageous. Outrageous marketing sells. It's memorable. It can get people talking about your business.

Consider Kentucky Fried Chicken. They had Colonel Sanders. Wendy's had Dave. Kinko's was named after its founder's kinky red hair. Crazy Eddie's Electronics became nationally famous because Eddie was—well, you get the picture, I hope.

Me? I've always been considered a fun guy. I love to make people laugh and I have a loose, happy style when I speak from the stage. So—instead of the usual three-piece power suit so many professional speakers will tell you are required, to "elevate" you above your audience, I always wear what I refer to as my "Florida Business Suit" when I speak or attend conferences and meetings. This is a high-quality Hawaiian-style shirt, dress slacks, and dress shoes—shirttail out.

Wearing this, I feel fun. I feel loose and happy (and comfortable). And it comes across in my delivery when I speak.

This process makes creating a strong memorable presence a lot easier. The process still boils down to a matter of trusting your gut and going with what you're comfortable with; but, if you're starting with the real *you*, this is easier than you might think. Still, getting to the real *you* sometimes takes a bit of help. That's what the survey is all about.

Easily Become More Memorable

I hear you again. (What *are* you doing—*thinking* out loud? Do you *read* out loud, too?) You're thinking—"If this is so easy, how come so few other businesses do it?"

The answer lies within human nature itself. We're all basically frightened, lonely individuals starving for acceptance, struggling to belong. From the first day we "earned" the wrath of our parents, we started building a natural desire to please people.

At a very early, impressionable age, we discovered that life is a lot easier when people like us and approve of what we do.

So—when it comes to our business personalities, we lean strongly toward the "safe" side. We try to "fit in," so we pattern ourselves after everyone else. We don't want to offend anyone. If someone is offended, they'll go away and not buy from us.

This can be a terrible mistake.

Trying to offend no one invariably dooms you to being like everyone else. You might fit in, but you'll never be remembered. There is no solidifying characteristic that your customers can be attracted to and identify with.

You become *forgettable*. Any customers that you eventually do attract to your business will be fleeting and fickle, easily led away from you again by someone offering lower prices or more selection.

Trying to please everyone rarely leads to any kind of sustainable success.

Pull your *real* character from the depths of your soul, blend that with some traits from your favorite TV character for additional identification power, and some people won't connect. They'll tune away. But some people *will* connect. These will be people who identify with you and like your persona—and they'll attach suction cups and hold on for the whole ride, defending their favorite "personality" business with a passion you can't buy.

You will become a part of these customers' lives—a part they look forward to visiting often.

Developing a personality for your business is a key to outselling *any* competitor you might tackle or who might choose to tackle you. We live in an experience economy. People want more than just the things you have to sell. They want to *feel* something while they're buying from you.

Developing a persona—a character—for your business, then positioning your business around that character, can enable you to sell the same things a competitor sells, at prices higher than your competitor charges, to customers who resonate with you, identify with your personality, and who would prefer to buy what they want from you.

If, for any reason, you still feel at all uncomfortable displaying the "real you," out for the public to see, an alternative solution might be to create an alter ego.

A Big-Assed Idea

I capitalized on the concept of outrageous marketing through the use of an alter ego when I launched *Big Profits TV*, the Internet marketing TV show I post regularly on the Web to promote myself and my business.

I knew I wanted a web address for the show that would be easy to remember. I also knew I needed one that suited my fun-loving nature. I couldn't believe my luck when I discovered that www.BigAssProfits .com was available.

I've been told by a few people that they simply can't promote a web address with the word "ass" in it. And I've been advised by a few of my clients that they would prefer that I change the address to something else.

I ignored them all. But, to soften the blow, I created a sidekick. My sidekick is a donkey. His name is Jack.

Jack's already taken up a life of his own. I receive e-mails addressed to Jack with suggestions of things for him to do on future shows. They're getting involved and, in today's online marketing world, everything should be focused on involving your prospects and clients, one way or an other.

One client suggested that I needed to differentiate between myself and Jack so there was no confusion who the jackass on the show really was (great advice I would never have thought of myself). So, I "taught" Jack to talk. This way, he could introduce me at the opening of the show, clearly drawing that much-needed line between the two of us.

This led to a movie I created about Jack's life. It tells the story of where he was born, his family life on the farm, why he ran away to join the circus, and how he met me and eventually became the featured mascot on the show.

You can see the whole seven-minute video epic on www
.BigAssProfits.com.

While you watch this movie, keep in mind that I produced everything you're seeing by myself. On a personal computer. And I shot all
the video with a Sony Handycam.

It's a good example of outrageous marketing gone wild, a nice mix
of company branding and the addition of a sidekick as a personality
to a business. I hope it also inspires you because that video wasn't
hard to create. It took a considerable amount of time but, thanks to
the wonders of today's available technology—the same blessing that
makes self-publishing so easy today—all the tools are very inexpensive, easy to use, and fairly easy to master.

Now that I've created the character of Jack and built his life story—
he's off and running (pardon the pun). And Jack is also the *perfect*
character to say things on the show that I might not want to say
myself.

It's usually better if you can bring out your own inner character and
use it. Sometimes, circumstances dictate that you create a sidekick or
alter ego character to accomplish the same goal. Whatever you do—I
highly recommend that you start creating a persona.

We're going to roll up our sleeves and start working on an e-book
and e-zine soon, and it's going to help make those tasks a lot easier
and bunches of fun when you do.

FUN MONEY PROFILE

Jorge Arguello

United Arts Movement International, Inc.
www.uami.org

Previous jobs held: There have been many because, looking back
on it, I was searching for my true calling, my life's purpose, if you
will—and that took 40-some years. Some jobs that I held: paperboy,
computer electronics specialist, engineering technician, management
of several departments in the industry, farming, state employment,
teaching in the school system, and much more that I've already for-
gotten. I suppose it shows that I wasn't a very employable person. I'm
way too independent.

Least favorite thing about working for someone else: The feeling that I was under all the rules connected to that reality—time constraints, making someone else rich.

Favorite thing about working for someone else: That I could take a project and see it to its fruition and do it right. When I was given the leeway and trust to complete projects for my employers, it always made me feel empowered.

Single pivotal moment or thing that helped make the switch to pursuing a FUN Money lifestyle: This was a long process. I feel that when I left "society" and my big-money career to move to the mountains and live the life of a spiritual guru was a very pivotal moment in my life and its direction. After all is said and done, however, after I met Alan R. Bechtold and became his student, I realized the direction I was moving, and it put me on the path of a real Internet business. Also, when I attended a one-day seminar that the late Corey Rudl held in San Diego, I finally made the decision to quit all my day jobs, burn the bridges, and never look back. It was imperative that I meet Corey, for some reason. While there, we spoke. We were going to connect up to do business together. A week later he was dead. That profound moment had, and still has, a lasting, resounding effect on my life today.

Emotional reactions when making the decision to quit the day job: I was elated and never felt any fear about it. I asked myself the question, "If not now, when?"—and I knew it was the most important moment of my life. The scary part came later, when going through the ups and downs of being in business or creating your own business. Being a single father with high school kids, at the time, I knew I would succeed, and I promised myself that I would. Success, of course, comes in many forms and continues today.

Reaction of your friends, family, and loved ones to your decision: Reactions were varied but, by and large, I was supported. I was really only concerned about how my immediate and closest family members felt. They all know me and love me. My friends are still amazed that I've survived and made it after all these years, but it's also a lesson for them. Hopefully, they'll get something out of it, too—even if it's just inspiration.

Time required to attain the FUN Money lifestyle: This isn't easy to answer because I felt that I was already living a FUN Money lifestyle. But, after that liberating decision, everything has become FUN Money since that point—even though I was already having fun being an online entrepreneur. Remember—it all started almost 30 years ago and all the different steps led me to this point; it's all been fun, as far as I'm concerned.

What you do now: Today, I continue to learn and build my for-profit businesses, but my life's purpose is to bring life, love, and empowerment to children of all ages through artistic creative expression, a program I've created and am teaching through my Artistic Creative Expression Centers. My first center is here in my hometown, but my plans are to create more throughout the United States and the world. I'll have 200 centers around the globe in 10 years. Those are my dreams coming true.

Your life today: My life is filled with wonder and joy as my journey continues to unfold. I've been able to spend time with my children and watch them grow and be a part of their lives. That one fact has been and still is the most important to me. What is wealth if you can't live enjoying it or miss out on life in the process of getting it? Today, I can travel when I want, have the leisure time that I desire, play music with my band, Majical, and I thank my personal God for giving me the insight and the guts to follow my passionate dreams.

Advice for other FUN Money seekers: Realize who you are and what you really have always done at your core, then apply the necessary steps to achieve and accomplish it. There is no better feeling in the world than when you're doing what your highest self and life's purpose guides you to do, and to be.

Wrap-Up

- Do some easy online "espionage":
  - Visit some sites selling information and products within your subniche.
  - Become your competitors' customer.

- — Study what they do to attract customers, make sales, and follow through.
- — Look for ways you can improve on what they do.
- Do not focus on lower prices.
- What are your favorite TV shows?
- Any characters on these shows that you relate to?
- Get a caricature of you drawn—or use Photoshop or similar software to create one from a photograph.
- Get two or three people who like you to complete the six-question survey:
  - — What one *physical* feature of mine do you find most attractive?
  - — What *emotional* characteristic do you like most about me?
  - — What *spiritual* characteristic do you like most about me?
  - — What *one thing* (physical, emotional, or spiritual) do you wish I'd change?
  - — Describe me in *three words* or less.
  - — What TV character do I remind you of the most?
- Create a character that captures the inner you:
  - — Create a sidekick if your own persona isn't working.

CHAPTER 3

IT ALL STARTS WITH A BOOK

No, you never get any fun out of the things you haven't done.
—Ogden Nash

Launching your own information business starts with creating a book. When you first heard it, this probably frightened you more than you'll admit. Don't worry.

There are countless other ways to launch or build a business being touted on the Web—but my three-step system has worked without fail throughout my many years of online publishing and marketing—and you're going to need to put together a book, too, to get it all rolling.

Just remember—I'm going to show you how to do this the *easy* way. If you like to write—great. But, you can sometimes actually do more *without* writing a word.

You're also going to plan and launch an online newsletter (called an e-zine—pronounced "ee-zene"). I know—this is scary-sounding, too—but it's a *lot* more fun than you might imagine. Especially when you do it the simple, no-writing way that I suggest.

Your book will establish you as an expert and easily attract prospects to you with free and extremely low-cost marketing—online and offline. Your book will also lead everyone reading it to the natural conclusion that they want to know more—so many of your readers will then sign up for your newsletter. Your newsletter keeps you in your customers' and prospects' minds, enables you to easily build and maintain a rapport with your prospects and customers—and it enables you to *sell things* . . . the point of launching *any* business, online or offline, new or established.

Publishing is the simplest key to turning any interest you're truly passionate about into a cash-producing business. It's also the key to differentiating yourself in a crowded marketplace, beating the competition, and pulling in prospective customers like mad.

In short—the three-step formula I'm exploring with you here is the ultimate way to make FUN Money happen quickly and easily, at minimum cost. It might look "too simple," with only three basic steps— but I've spent the better part of 30 years developing it and testing it, based on my own experience.

I've never been able to find anything that works better for getting a new business started on the Web, then building it to a sustainable level. Every time a client has applied my simple formula to his or her brick-and-mortar business or existing online business, it's increased sales and made life a lot more fun for the owner in the process.

Even if you don't aspire to owning a successful business, my three-step formula will enable you to easily turn your favorite pastime into a perpetual motion machine that pays for itself and increases your enjoyment of whatever it is you love doing most.

FREE FUN IS GREAT FUN

Remember those first early video game machines? The Atari 2600? Intellivision? Colecovision? I fell in love with them. I was instantly *addicted*. But, I was also raising a family, working on my writing and publishing career, and being a househusband.

I definitely didn't have the money to spend on cartridges and machines.

Frustrated, I teamed up with a friend and we launched a newsletter, *The Logical Gamer*. We wrote to all the leading video game companies and we requested review copies.

It wasn't long before the review copies started coming in. More accurately, they *poured* in. Atari, Mattel, Activision, Coleco, and a host of third-party software developers were kicking out new game cartridges in droves . . . and they sent every new title they released directly to my door—*free*.

My partner and I went to the Consumer Electronics Show in Chicago that year and visited all the booths related to new video games. There were companies there we didn't even know existed. They all welcomed us with open arms, demonstrated prototypes of their newest games and machines, and treated us like VIPs—and they all put us on their review lists.

We never made any solid money with that newsletter. I think we broke even on the venture. But—we got literally *hundreds* of new video games, about half-a-dozen new home video game consoles, and we had a *ton* of fun pursuing our passion—*at no cost*.

Even better, because this venture was set up and run like a business, it was all tax-deductible fun.

This was before the Web or we might have been fine. We also failed to create a persona that video gamers could relate to, something to give our newsletter a memorable "hook." We also didn't use my three-step formula to promote our newsletter because I hadn't yet developed it fully.

As soon as I discovered the world of dial-up computer bulletin board systems (BBSs), I launched a news service and syndicated it to the operators of these systems.

The BBS operators (sysops) were all hobbyists at first. They ran their bulletin boards on spare computers, just for fun. As their hobbies started costing more and more money, a few brave souls started charging for access to their systems.

The news service I started, INFO-MAT, covered what's new in computers and software and on the bulletin boards. I sold exclusive territories on a monthly basis and, at one point, had more than 300 systems subscribing worldwide.

Once I was making money online, things changed. I didn't need to physically print my publications any more, saving me a huge amount of money and time. And there was no postage needed to deliver my publications. This represented yet another huge savings. Life was *good*.

Then, along came a new phenomenon known as CDs. Those little shiny discs we now routinely buy our music on.

I launched *Online Digital Music Review* and made it a part of my package of syndicated information that BBS sysops could buy to carry on their systems. I wrote to all the major record companies, told them about my new publication, told them I was reviewing *all* genres of music on CD, and requested review copies.

The parade of UPS, FedEx, and Airborne Express trucks began again. This time, they brought me free CDs, new boxed sets, and advance releases. The CDs came pouring in by the *hundreds*.

I made more money with INFO-MAT than I ever did publishing *Online Digital Music Review*—but, again, I'd tapped online publishing to turn a passion into money by *eliminating* the cost of building a huge collection of music on CD. And, this time, I did it online, so it cost me virtually nothing.

This is simply something I've always done. Even when I couldn't get someone to buy what I wrote, I found early on that I could publish it myself. And as long as I wrote about something I loved doing, the worst I could do was enjoy what I loved doing even more, at low cost or no cost. And I was able to write off whatever small costs I did incur from my taxes.

This can work for you, too—because it can work for *anyone*.

MAIL BOXED IN

Robert Imbriale, author of *Motivational Marketing*, is a great friend and brilliant marketing expert. I highly recommend his book when you're ready to grow your business with some truly powerful marketing that's easy and inexpensive to do.

Robert tells the story of the man who owned one of those quick printing and mailing shops in his area. Robert always used the shop to get printing done and to handle his shipping needs. One day, he went into the shop, and there was a trashcan lying up against the wall, its contents spilling out. From the back of the shop, he could hear the owner, normally a very happy-go-lucky service-oriented guy, slamming things around and grumbling to himself, obviously unhappy.

When he noticed Robert standing at the counter, he came out of the back room, still looking dour.

Robert asked him what was up. He confessed he was sick and tired of running his business. He was tired of dealing with demanding customers who didn't appreciate him when he went the extra mile, he couldn't get his employees to come in on time, and usually found himself constantly filling in at the counter for no-shows.

It was killing him.

Robert started working with this man and found out his true passion, the one thing he lived for, was skiing.

The whole reason he started the business he was running was to free up enough time and money to ski more often. Instead, he'd found himself tied to the shop, working more hours than he ever wanted to, and making less money than he'd hoped in return.

Robert helped this frustrated entrepreneur start a newsletter about skiing. He also set up a web site. Now, the man spends all of his time seeking out the next great ski lodge, rating the slopes, testing new equipment—and telling the readers of his newsletter about what he's found.

He's doing this full-time. The revenue has replaced what he was making at the print shop, and he now does what he always loved doing most, full-time.

This wasn't a *writer*. Robert showed him how to publish a newsletter *without* having to be a writer—just as I'm showing you.

PLOTTING YOUR NEW LIFE

By now you should be fully aware of my plan. I'm going to turn you into a publisher. You don't have any idea how—yet—but that's okay because you're doing the work required to get there, possibly without realizing it.

You've researched your interests to discover your true passion, you've investigated the shared interest in your passion online, you've looked into some of your potential competitors, and you've started laying the groundwork of branding your new home-based online publishing business.

Next, we need to put this all into a plan you can easily follow.

Without a plan, you *will* surprise yourself with where you wind up, most every time. Unfortunately, surprises in business are almost *never* a good thing.

Look at your business like you would look at a car trip with the family. Would you load everyone up, throw some stuff in the trunk, rough-and-tumble, then head out to see where you wind up?

Forget your carefree youth, when "road trip" was a war cry of independence and planning was *not* what independence was all about. This is your *family* we're talking about here—even if you have to imagine one to bring this example to life. I don't care how good you are at parenting, there's no way your kids will ever accept an answer of "I don't know" when they ask their favorite question, "Are we there yet?"

Believe it or not, a *lot* of people start businesses with no more planning than you used to do when you "planned" a road trip in your college days.

Instead—decide where you would like to be with your business by the end of year one. Then, set another goal for year two. Some experts suggest that you plan out five years in advance, but I've never found that to be practical or required—unless you intend to go after investors or a bank loan.

Fortunately, the way we're going to start your business, you won't need investors unless and until you're truly ready for them and already making great money. Then, you *might* want to go after investors, to grow your business to the next level and make even more money.

But—we'll worry about that then. It's not at all required to get your new FUN Money life plotted out now.

If you stick with the steps I'm spelling out for you here, you probably won't need much money to get started at all—if any. Because you won't need investors, you only need to plan the first couple of years out.

Believe me, you'll want to at least plan that far ahead. Setting a goal for each of the next two years gives you two destination points.

Think Two Years Ahead

Get out a two-year calendar (use one on your computer, if you wish). Mark your two destination points.

When setting your goals—the destination points you're aiming for—decide how much money you want to be making as you arrive at your destination, the number of employees you anticipate you'll need by then, and any expanded needs to accommodate a staff and what you intend to be doing with your business by then. Make sure you include offices, equipment, and so on.

This will tell you how much money you need to bring into your business to reach your goals. Feel free to think a bit ambitiously. Divide the total amount you figure you'll need by 365 and write that amount on each day, leading back to today.

Now you know, each day, how much you need to make in order to achieve your goal. Once you've decided on your main product, determined your cost to deliver that product to the customer, and what your profit will be, you'll also know how many products you need to sell each day to get to your destination.

It's like deciding how far you can drive in a day so you can book a motel room that'll be waiting for you and your family when you arrive at each stopping point in your trip.

This is an *extremely* simplistic approach. Much more so than any business plan you've probably seen or read about in any book about planning a small business. But I've seen far too many people get bogged down in the planning stages of starting a business—and I don't want to see you stop before you've even begun.

If you just follow the steps I've outlined, you'll be able to knock out your plan quickly and start moving forward. You'll have a lot more direction and focus. This will enable you to start planning, each day, the steps you need to take to sell the number of products you know you need to sell, so you can stay on track.

You'll also know when you're offtrack, so you know what you need to do to get back on the road to your destination.

You can also adjust your sales figures each day. For example, you know you won't sell as many products the first three months as you will the second three, after you've had more time to build your business. Just *lower* the daily assumption for those first three months and spread the remaining sales out over the remaining year, if you need to.

I plot out a simple 365-day split over each day, then keep a count of the "shortage" as I grow my sales—then I spread that shortage out over the remaining days in the year as I move through each month.

On good years, I get to do this in *reverse*.

Hot Resource

Go to www.FUNdamentalYou.com. You'll find a free downloadable calendar program there that you can install on your computer. You can use this calendar to easily set up your plan for as many years out as you care to go, plus you can use the system to track all your appointments, your to-do items, and a whole lot more.

You'll love it, and the price is certainly right. It's free.

After you've set your one- and two-year goals, go back and *double* them. The key is to think *big*. Aim *high*. Even if you think you plan to stay with a small, home-based business the rest of your life, "supersizing" your goals will help you hit them more than anything else I can possibly recommend.

Value of Thinking Big

I once set up a whole plan to generate more than $1 million in online sales in a single day. Internet marketing expert John Reese had, a few months prior, set the record for this at $1.2 million. I followed all the steps he followed and set up a similar promotional system building toward a one-day-only special offer. I worked hard to line up several other friends in the business to help promote the special offer. Then, I headed off to a workshop I was conducting that same weekend.

During the workshop, I routinely checked in on sales—live, in front of my students.

I was fully prepared to hit the goal or at least to do very well. Part of my plan was to let my students see the results, real time, before their very eyes.

Apparently, a much larger percentage of the marketers Reese worked with during his promotion actually promoted his offer leading up to the sale. I'm fairly certain Reese also wasn't preparing for a three-day workshop while he was setting up his launch effort.

My bad. I only made $65,000 in sales that day. This was a *miserable* failure when you consider my goal of selling *more* than $1.2 million in a day. Still, it was a *great* day by anybody's usual standards. When was the last time you made $65,000 in one day?

But—if I'd set out with a goal of hitting only $65,000 in a day, I would only have worked that hard. I would have only set things up with that goal in mind. Instead, because I pushed myself harder than I'd ever pushed before, truly aiming at that $1.2 million + goal, even my miss was very nice.

Wouldn't *you* like to "fail" by making *only* $65,000 in *one day*? Instead of a "miserable failure," I call that a "*magnificent* failure."

Change Will Become a Constant

Your plan is going to change, anyway. This is the *only* way planning your business differs from planning a road trip with the family. When you map out that family car trip, Orlando isn't going to suddenly pick up and relocate halfway across the country in the other direction.

Chances are good it'll stay put right where it is in Florida, awaiting your arrival.

Your goals for your business, unlike Orlando, will constantly change as you move forward. This is why I never advise anyone to start a business by mapping out goals, in detail, for the next five years. You need a plan, but you also need to keep that plan flexible. Realize it will need to be constantly revisited and revised, depending on what happens along the road.

Focus on planning just enough that you always have an answer for "Are we there yet?" and you'll be head-and-shoulders ahead of almost everyone else starting a business.

STORYBOARDING YOUR NEW LIFE: IT'S LIKE PLANNING A SCREENPLAY—BUT A *LOT* EASIER

Now that you have your basic long-term plan in place, your next step is setting up a systemized way to "fill in the gaps." This is where you start establishing the procedures you'll use to make the daily sales in that plan happen.

You'll use this system a *lot* more as you get closer to actually launching your business. The instructions for setting this up are here, however, because you'll find places along the path where you'll want to start mapping out all the smaller steps that are in each of the three basic steps to my formula.

MBA courses and most business books would simply call this "product development planning," "business launch planning," or "promotional planning." I've found it's easier to envision each product and promotion you map out as if you're "scripting" the steps. That's why I refer to it as "product development storyboarding," "business launch storyboarding," and "promotional storyboarding."

Video producers use storyboards to map out each scene in a production. Finished professional storyboards look like a comic book, with each scene or camera shot illustrated, plus instructions on how the shot should look and what the actors in each scene should do.

For your purposes, your "movie" would be a plan for putting together a new information product, steps you need to take to put together an e-book, the specific steps for setting up and publishing your newsletter, or the steps required to put together any marketing push.

If you're absolutely married to the computer and can't think of doing anything without having your computer help you with the task, you can download some excellent free storyboarding software at www.FUNdamentalYou.com. There is a Windows version and two Mac versions. There are also excellent instructions on using the storyboarding software—although it's so easy to use you will probably never need the instructions.

Storyboarding software makes this process easy and fun. Just ignore all the references to video production, camera angles, and so on in the software and use each frame to describe *one step* in your product launch, business launch, or marketing plan.

I like using storyboarding software because, just like your initial rough business plan, lots of things will change. Storyboarding software makes it easy to shuffle your plan, rearrange it, add to it or delete from it, and still maintain a full view of the big picture.

You could do the same thing with the free calendar software I told you about earlier. Or a simple text file. The text file just won't give you the "big picture" the way a storyboard or calendar will—and it's tougher to change things around as conditions change.

If you prefer working with pen and ink, 3 × 5 cards can substitute for a planner or storyboarding software. I like this organizational method because it's available even when a computer isn't handy. The cards are easy to sort and re-sort at will, it's easy to add steps on the cards or to simply start a new card, and you can "delete" any cards that you no longer need by simply pitching them into any handy trashcan.

Also, 3 × 5 cards fit easily in your pocket. A computer can get a bit cramped in there.

Create one file folder for your business plan. Create another file folder for your marketing plan. Then, create a separate file folder for each new product you plan to produce. I would suggest you create one of each to start with.

Each task goes on a 3 × 5 card that is then stored in the appropriate folder. Whenever you want to add to your to-do list, you pull out the 3 × 5 cards you have, sort through them, and determine if you have a substep (something needed to get the step you started on a card done) or a new step.

Substeps go on existing cards. New steps get a new card.

This is just a simple system of to-do lists that are easy to re-arrange, add to or subtract from as you go along. I don't recommend you simply use to-do lists, however. The tasks I've just outlined are even more important than your business plan, which was simply a skeleton idea to follow, your overall map to where you're eventually going. The steps you need to actually take to achieve your plan are so much more important I recommend you go the *extra* mile when mapping them out.

A final note on the file folders: You only need one business plan folder. You probably noticed I also told you to make only one marketing plan folder, but to create a separate folder for each product you decide to launch.

Why not create a separate marketing plan folder for each product? Marketing is not something that you do separately for each product you have. You'll start out with one product. Soon, you'll be adding more. As you add more products, your marketing plan will change, but it should still be organized as a single, complete system, so one product sale can naturally lead to another and another.

A Fluid Marketing System Makes Additional Sales Happen

The easiest sale you'll ever make (beyond anything you give away for free to attract prospects to your business in the first place) is additional sales to customers after they've already purchased something from you. After we've launched your business with the three-step system in place and a single product to sell, we'll start adding more products. You'll want to tie your existing marketing plan into each new product you sell, so you create a virtual funnel through which your prospects will move, leading up to the ultimate conclusion to buy from you, at the maximum possible price point.

In Jenny's case, she's decided to start with a free e-book about finding and caring for rare collectible Barbies. This will lead people to sign up for the newsletter she'll also begin publishing, about collecting rare Barbies.

We haven't discussed it yet, but I have the added advantage of being able to read ahead in the script, so I know she's going to choose to start creating some original Barbie clothes, in the tradition of the originals when they were released, specially designed for rare collectible Barbies. For now, Jenny's going to sign up for an affiliate program with one of her competitors and sell their clothes.

73

Jenny's funnel looks like this:

- Free e-book—the mouth of the funnel—the widest point where prospects will come into her business, read what she has to say, and, then sign up for her free newsletter to keep hearing from Jenny.
- Free newsletter—the next step moving through the funnel. It's a bit narrower because not everyone who takes Jenny's free e-book will sign up for the newsletter.
- In the newsletter, Jenny will intersperse her expertise and opinions with occasional offers to buy some of the clothing in the affiliate program she signed up for. Since the company she'll be promoting sells high-quality machine-made Barbie clothing, and only a certain percentage of her newsletter readers will buy them, this is represented by a still-narrower portion of the funnel.
- Moving down the funnel, Jenny plans to also make original, handmade, authentic Barbie clothes for rare collectible Barbie dolls available. These are much higher-priced, one-of-a-kind pieces, and they will sell for many times the price of the more-standard machine-made clothing offered in her affiliate program. This product represents the narrowest part of her marketing funnel.

Four different products. Four different levels of interest. One train leading to all the stations, pulling prospects with it all the way. *All* of Jenny's marketing needs to be focused on aiming for people interested in her e-book, then leading them through a process of getting to know and trust Jenny better, so they start buying what she recommends.

The biggest money will be made at the smallest end of the funnel, where Jenny will eventually see high-end customers buying her original creations.

In the end, however, it's all one single marketing system.

Adjusting the Profit Picture

If you prefer, you can think of your marketing funnel as a distillery. It might help make the entire process easier for you to see—and it'll *definitely* make it more fun. Then, you would consider the free e-book the water or soda, and the free newsletter as the sugar. The articles and offers you put into the newsletter, then, would be the yeast and malt.

On the other end, you get beer, then wine, then cognac, then spirits.

Just get some 3 × 5 cards and file folders, mark the file folders as I've instructed for now, and put them all in the file drawer.

Or get the storyboard software and start using it.

Next, we'll move back into some branding steps. Again, branding is optional. But, if you skip it, getting your new business off the ground and growing will likely require a bit more effort.

CASTING CALL: PLUGGING IN YOUR CHARACTER

At this point, you'll want to start fleshing out your business character some more. I went with a simple, easy-going, Hawaiian shirt-wearing me for my *Bit Profits* TV show. Then, I added Jack, the donkey, for good measure. Benjamin Franklin is involved in a new project I'm working on (yes—historical figures are fine if they *fit*). I'll tell you more about The Franklin Guild later in this book.

Jenny's going to go with her red hair and freckles as branding elements. She didn't go to a caricature artist like I suggested—he wasn't on the corner the two days she tried visiting where he usually works. But, she did the alternative: she found a photo she could render as a "stamp" in Photoshop.

Any good photo retouching software can usually be used to turn a photo of yourself into either a line drawing or a painting or rubber stamp. This will make your photo look like art. It won't be quite as good as a caricature, but it will work fine.

Caricature artists are great for creating a persona for your business, but if you don't have access to one, don't let that slow you down. Use Photoshop or a similar graphics editing program and an interesting filter to create a caricature on your own. Or you can use a service such as www.funfaces.com to obtain a caricature drawing from a photo, which is also a great option.

Next, we did a bit of word association. I suggested we focus on Jenny's hair as a place to begin. This led us to:

- Cherries
- Apples

- Strawberries
- Licorice
- Fire trucks (you should throw *every* idea on the table because you never know when an idea will grow on you)
- Fire

Next, we worked on associating the red words with Barbie, creating a solid tie-in between Jenny's business persona, her caricature, and her market.

Jenny liked "The Apple of Barbie's Eye."

I liked it, too, but I wasn't ready to stop there. Giving it some more thought, I came up with "Strawberry Barbies Forever." (I told you I was a Beatles fan.)

I forgot Jenny was too young to have grown up with the Beatles phenomenon. Still, many of her potential clients were my age. They'd dig it.

Jenny was unmoved.

Finally, after a *lot* of word juggling, we decided to go with "Forever Barbie." It wasn't even *close* to what we started out aiming for. It didn't even *hint* at the red-haired creator's complexion and glowing red crown of hair. But, it resonated with the focus of Jenny's business and prospects more, so we decided to run with it.

To round it all out and make it fit, we also decided to go with a general strawberry red theme to her business (red business cards, order forms, web site backgrounds—you name it)—and to use her stylized photo as the "Aunt Jemima" of her business—the character related to her business.

Jenny gave the character she decided would replace herself the name Strawbarbie Fields. I thought that was a nice touch.

Now Jenny was free to start building a story around this Strawbarbie Fields character, like I did with Jack, the donkey, on my Internet TV show. Jenny chose to write out a brief story, leaving a lot of unexplained mystery that she felt would appeal to Barbie fans.

Who was I to argue? I'm not a Barbie fan. I have no idea what would intrigue them most—but Jenny sure does. That's the power of setting up a business around what you love doing most. You *are* your customers, so you know what will make them react positively or negatively.

The Story of Strawbarbie Fields

Strawbarbie Fields was once a Barbie doll herself. When Jenny was a very young girl, she found her in her mom's strawberry patch. She was all dirty, and her clothes were ruined by the rain and mud, so Jenny brought her in, cleaned her up, and named her.

Over the next few months, Jenny worked long and hard to create a complete, authentic-looking outfit of clothes for her new best friend. The moment she put them on her, the doll came to life—and they've remained best friends ever since.

Now Jenny's devoted her life to making certain that all Barbie dolls everywhere are properly outfitted with clothes that match the *original* clothes they were wearing when they were sold, so they can always be fresh and sparkling clean, ready to be some girl's best friend, too.

In short—she's determined to bring as many neglected classic Barbie dolls to life as she can.

Strawbarbie Fields now works in Jenny's shop, advising her, so the story goes, to make certain that her hand-sewn designs are authentic to the originals down to the last detail.

It's far-fetched. But, it also captures much of the wonder and beauty of that special relationship between a girl and a doll. This makes perfect sense, since Jenny's target audience is an older, affluent woman who fondly remembers her own experience growing up with Barbie and who wants to continue to enjoy that experience by collecting Barbies today.

Naturally, some of these women will want authentic replacement clothing for their collections—to "bring their dolls to life." Jenny will be there, ready to provide them.

Note that Jenny never quite explains how Strawbarbie Fields came to life and started working in her shop—beyond the "magic" of putting on that first authentic-looking outfit. That's some of the mystique she'll reveal over the next few months as she opens her business, launches her newsletter, and starts pulling people in. The story will be the connector that pulls her prospects and customers together with her, forming an impenetrable bond no competitor will easily break.

For now, just remember—if I can teach a donkey to talk, Jenny has every right to bring a favorite Barbie from her childhood to life.

Follow through the process with your own character—or caricature, or sidekick or alter ego. Build your character and see how you can tie it to your business in a way that makes sense. Remember that the idea is to make your business instantly memorable, so it stands head-and-shoulders above any potential competitors that you'll have to go up against or that might come along after you've built your business and have things rolling.

Your caricature and her story should resonate with your target audience. It doesn't have to be funny or cute, like Jack or Strawbarbie—but it most certainly can be, if that fits your own personality.

CHARACTERS COUNT

For example—I was talking to one of the leaders of a network marketing company I've been working with recently. He told me about one member of his downline who called up, excited, telling him he should go look at the new video he'd just posted on YouTube.

My friend watched the video. He was *shocked. Aghast.*

"The guy was sitting there, on camera, smoking a cigarette—wearing *shades*," he said. "He told people to just stop asking questions and get into this opportunity and, if they needed any information, call the number on the screen."

"Alan," he said, desperation and fear glistening in his eyes. "The guy looked Jack Nicholson *scary*—and that was *my* number he put up on that screen for people to call."

I asked him if anyone called.

"That's the amazing part. I'm getting more calls from that guy's video than I'm getting from any of my other team members."

I love this story. It proves my point that being yourself will hook people in who resonate with you. It will also literally force them to want to do business with you and no one else. I hate to imagine why those people resonated with that guy's video. But—they *called*. And this guy was getting more action than any of the other people in my friend's network marketing downline.

Remember what I said. Being yourself *will* chase some people away. But it will also resonate so deeply with *other* people—those people who most closely identify with you—that you will appear to them as exactly what they've been looking for. They'll not only do business with you, they will *prefer* doing business with you over any potential competitor—even if that competitor is selling the same thing for *less money.*

It would appear there are some other "Jack Nicholson scary" people out there who resonated with my friend's teammate. Bully for him. I calmed my friend down when I reminded him that Jack Nicholson scary or not, if he was building the team, it didn't matter.

Just don't fake it. That *never* works. If you're a deadpan serious analytical sort, pull out a slide rule and *analyze* your way through your sales pitch. If you're fun-loving, have *fun*.

A Super Profitable Superhero

I recently met Daryn Ross at a workshop where I was teaching. Daryn owns a sourcing business for business specialties companies. He's the one who gets those hats, pens, cups, T-shirts, and mouse pads (or anything else you might imagine), that companies emblazon with logos and clever sayings.

Daryn started his business in his college dorm more than 19 years ago, and he's grown it into a multimillion-dollar company today. He explained to me that what he sells is a commodity. Most of his competitors all try to undercut each other on price. He decided, instead, to go for a different angle, so he focused on superfast service. This was something the entire industry was constantly crying out for, so this became his selling point, his company's "personality."

He named his company Megafast. Their unique selling position is superfast service that no one can beat.

But he didn't stop there. He wanted to make this unique selling position truly memorable in the minds of his customers and prospects—so he also created a superhero character—Mega Man.

Now, when you visit his company's web site at www.megafastline .com, you can see Mega Man smiling at you from the top left corner of the page. Then, you hear an exhilarating "*Whoosh*," and a heavy, echoing voice booms out, "Welcome to Megafast—Experience the rush."

Yes—it's Daryn wearing the Spandex suit and smiling from the top of the page. He also wears the outfit at trade shows where his company displays its services. And he's kicking *butt* in an overcrowded industry that's totally focused on cutting prices.

Daryn also won the coveted Glazer/Kennedy Marketer of the Year award in 2007, competing against several other companies.

I hear all the time that silly doesn't sell. This is usually sage advice—from someone who is too uptight to wear tights. Don't fall for it. Be glad most businesses have bought into this myth. Find yourself a unique angle and silly it up if you can. If that's *you*.

Or find someone else willing to do it for you.

Skip this step at your own peril. There are *tons* of businesses that have. Many are doing okay, but, if you want to stand out and *guarantee* your success in this time when everyone is overexposed to literally hundreds, if not thousands of marketing messages per day, get bold. Be daring. There is no easier way to accomplish this than by being *you*. Yes—it's possible to take it too far. But, you never know until you try.

Taking It Too Far

Not long ago, a car dealership known for outrageous behavior announced a " 'Jihad on car prices' sale." Someone leaked to the media that the company was planning to have all of its salespeople wear burkahs for the sale—and they were going hand out free toy swords to the kids who came in with their folks.

This was too far over the top, obviously. They hit a sore nerve with Americans who are already up-in-arms about anything relating to Muslim extremists. I don't imagine most Muslims were too pleased to hear about the dealers' plans, either.

The story spread over the newswires, hitting all the national news services. The parent company called and told the dealer it wouldn't stand for it, so the campaign was canceled. It should have been.

But—just look at the *free publicity* they generated.

Be creative. Step right up to the line without stepping over, remain sensitive to people's feelings and current events, and it's entirely possible to get that kind of coverage *without* the outrage.

You can do it. With a bit of research, planning, and a bit of luck, you could just come up with something that gets the world talking about you. Talk is cheap, and word-of-mouth marketing is the best deal on earth for any business.

BE YOUR OWN NIELSEN—FINDING OUT WHAT YOUR PROSPECTS WANT TO BUY BEFORE YOU SPEND ONE MINUTE DEVELOPING ANYTHING

Now we're going to do a bit more *fun* research, before actually getting into the nitty-gritty of setting up your business and getting it rolling.

Your goal, before selecting your products and creating your e-book and newsletter, is to find out exactly what the ideal prospect for your business wants to know more about.

It helps a *lot* if you're your own best customer. Again, this is why it's always best to build a business around something you love doing and already know something about.

My friend, T. J. Rohleder, cofounder of M.O.R.E. Inc. (Mid-American Opportunity Research Enterprises), was always a big fan of home business opportunities. He tells the story of when he was a carpet cleaner, with one broken-down truck, shlepping the muck out of people's carpets for a living.

He spent every spare dime he had buying one home business opportunity program after another, until he'd bought *hundreds* of them.

None worked, until he found one that he thought *might* work—*if* he modified it slightly first.

He and his wife, Eileen, made some small changes to the program. Then, they wrote a small booklet called "Dialing for Dollars." T. J. sold his carpet cleaning van to raise the $300 he needed to place an ad in one of the business opportunity magazines—and the rest is history.

Today, he's generated more than $100 *million* in sales selling home business opportunities—and he's helped create dozens of millionaires in the process.

T. J. was his own best customer. He knew his prospects inside and out because all he had to do was look within himself to find the answers to his questions about what his customers and prospects were most looking for—then create it and sell it to them.

Even if you're your own best customer, however, it's still best to also do a bit more investigating to see what your prospects are *currently* looking for.

The easiest way to do this research is with online forums.

Quietly Listen—And Take Notes

Online forums are places where people with similar interests gather online to discuss their favorite pastimes and pleasures, swap ideas and get to know one another. Today, these are referred to as Web 2.0 "community" sites, but I've always known them as forums and that's what I'm going to keep calling them.

There are tens of thousands of online forums available today, covering literally every topic imaginable. Including quite a few topics you wouldn't even *want* to imagine.

The secret to finding forums is simple. Just visit your favorite search engine and type in any keyword related to your chosen niche or subniche, followed by the word "forum." You'll see *hundreds*, if not *thousands* of forums listed. Dozens at a minimum.

I just typed "camel breeding forum" into Google, for example, and got back nearly 45,000 results. I'm certain most don't have anything to do with camel breeding—but there were some. When I typed in "Barbie forum" for Jenny, Google returned more than 3.5 *million* results.

Not *all* of those results will actually be forums about the subject you're interested in. But the first few pages usually are—and that's more than enough to do your next research step.

After you've found a few good forums, sign up for five or six. Register and visit them daily. Give them 15 to 30 minutes each per day. If a particular forum has no new posts within a day or two, join one of the others you've found until you're only on forums with activity.

Remember that you will likely find your subniche dealt with as a subject or "thread" within niche forums covering a larger interest area, so don't forget to pull back to your niche, rather than your subniche, if you need to find more forums for this step.

Look at each forum's different message categories to find ones closely associated with your subniche, settle in and start reading everyone's posts on the subject.

Forum users call this "lurking," and it's perfectly acceptable behavior. This provides you with the equivalent of sitting in a quiet bar near a packed table filled with prospective customers, all loudly discussing their most pressing needs—*while you take notes.*

Jenny looked on the Barbie and doll forums we found for such categories as "clothes," "handmade clothes," "authentic clothes," "collecting," "rare Barbies"—that sort of thing. She watched for comments from forum members that expressed a problem she knew she could solve with her business. When she found one, she wrote it down.

You should do this on the forums you've found, too.

If you can't find any discussions that help your research into what your prospects would want most, it's probably time to go back and do a little more niche research.

Introduce yourself on the forum in the category most closely tied to your business. Offer an answer or two to some questions posed by other forum users. Or just post some interesting information you've learned or known for years.

You only need to hone in on one or two forums with this approach. Abandon the forums that never seem to have any meaningful posts and simply narrow in on the one or two that do.

Online forums aren't referred to as online communities for nothing. The people who visit and participate in forums are all passionate about the subject, but they're also human beings who long to associate with like-minded people. Introduce yourself and bring value to the community by offering your help and advice and whatever knowledge you have, and you'll soon find forum members turning to you for answers and looking up to you as a valued member.

This is the perfect time to start asking the forum members to tell you what's *really* on their minds. After you've laid the necessary groundwork, you can feel free to tell members of your chosen forum or forums that you're launching a new business and you'd like to know what they most want to know and buy.

Here are a few questions that should get things started for you:

- What tools or information have you had the hardest time finding?
- What *one thing* would make your hobby more fun?
- What's your *biggest* gripe about the suppliers you currently buy from? (No names, please—this isn't a "bash the other guys" session, but a serious fact-finding mission I need help with.)
- What one thing do you like most about the supplier you currently buy from most often? (Again—no names—this isn't an advertising session, either.)

Feel free to word your questions exactly the way I have them stated, or alter them to suit your needs.

Easily Taking Your Research to a Higher Level

The more information you can gather about your prospects, *before* you launch your business, the better your chances of success will be. Monitoring and participating in a couple of popular forums, *listening* to the participants and asking them a few pointed questions, can easily be all the research you need to start a FUN Money business the right way.

But—when it comes to prelaunch intelligence, more is definitely better. After you get yourself established on a quality forum, tell the participants you're launching a new business and you want to make absolutely certain that it serves every forum member's needs better than anyone else has or could. Then, ask them to visit a web address and fill out a short survey to help you.

Here's an easy, *free* way to set up a genuine online survey capable of asking up to 10 questions: visit www.SurveyMonkey.com. This is a free online survey system that allows you to set up surveys with up to 10 questions and allows up to 100 people to take the survey. All with point-and-click ease. They host the survey, and the system provides you with *automatic* reports that show the answers, making it easy for you to determine the results in a flash.

You can also elect to pay $19.95 per month. This will provide you with the ability to create expanded surveys, choose from more ready-to-use survey templates, and allow up to 1,000 people respond.

You can do all the research you need to find out what your marketplace is looking for with Survey Monkey's free service. Twenty *honest* responses can tell you a lot—if you ask the right questions. A hundred responses would be great. Surveys will continue to come in handy as you grow your business, and you should use them any time you feel the need to check the pulse of your market because that pulse, like your goals, will change from time to time.

You should consider signing up for Survey Monkey's monthly service eventually. Definitely give the free service a try, get used to the system, and start planning ways you can use it later.

PLANNING THE HAPPY ENDING

We've now discussed all the preliminary steps we had to take before you could start your business. This planning and preparation will give your business the greatest chance to generate a *ton* of FUN Money, without the usual headaches experienced by so many entrepreneurs who don't properly plan ahead.

I also warned you to keep your job until we get things rolling because there are no instant answers. Despite the frequency with which you hear it repeated over and over again online and offline, most "overnight successes" take *years* of groundwork to happen. My system is extremely fast and easy—but it's not instant.

Sorry. I wish we could just pop a business into the microwave and churn out a winner in days—but it simply doesn't happen that way.

Work through the steps and you'll be surprised how much fun they are. You'll also find yourself gaining a newfound appreciation of your favorite activity as you discover other people who also enjoy it and delve into their interests and focus. And you'll find that the time required to complete these steps flies.

I also promised that, soon, you'd be diving into the meat of getting your business up and running.

One Final Preliminary Step

We're *about* to begin. There is only one more step you need to take before we start putting together the first plank of your three-step business-building system.

Take a look at the answers to your questions on the forums. Or, study the postings you found that provided you with answers. Or look over the survey you sent to members of the forums. Look for clues. What information do they most want? What services are they seeking? What ways can you set up your business so that it provides what other businesses in your chosen niche don't?

Jenny learned that her instincts were right on target. Collectors were most eager to find truly *faithful* reproductions of *original* Barbie outfits so they could dress their collectible dolls in the most authentic manner possible.

She also discovered that the current line of machined Barbie clothes she was planning to sell were popular among collectors— but many serious collectors were also more than willing to spend a *lot* more for carefully crafted, true-to-the-original reproductions of vintage Barbie clothes.

Another interesting thing we learned as a result of Jenny's research was directly related to the information collectors wanted and couldn't find anywhere. They wanted details about the original clothes that vintage Barbies came with, and the outfits that were available options at the time they were originally being sold in the stores.

Jenny also learned that serious Barbie collectors often *removed* the original outfits that were on their dolls and stored them. They would rather dress them in inferior imitations for everyday display than expose their original outfits to the effects of humidity and age. They expressed a need for information on the best ways to preserve those original outfits—and supplies to help them put them away safely.

When we discussed the results of her research, Jenny was surprised at how closely she'd already pegged the market. "This is incredible," she said. "I knew those were *my* biggest problems, and I *thought* I'd picked the right thing to sell them—but I had no idea other people felt the same way."

"That's the value of knowing your market," I told her. "Focusing on the thing you love doing most makes knowing your market much easier."

I paused a moment for effect. Then, I added, "I hope you also realize this proves you're much more of an expert in your field than you ever imagined."

She was dumfounded, but she reluctantly agreed.

Now Jenny knows she's qualified to position herself as an expert among Barbie collectors. After all, she's been collecting them most of her life. She also knows how she's going to position the new business she wants to build—and she knows what many serious collectors most want.

Jenny's ready to roll—are you?

Many people find it hard to accept the fact they could be seen as an expert to someone else. If this is still holding you back, you *might* not be focusing in on the right niche, something you truly love doing. Reexamine your research and realize you *are* an expert. Everyone is an expert at *something*. A lot of the groundwork I've had you doing so far is geared toward helping you find that "something" you're most qualified to help other people learn.

When you position yourself as an expert, people will learn a lot more willingly from you—and you'll sell a *lot* more of whatever it is you want to sell.

And—the very best way in the world to establish yourself as an expert, in any market, is—to publish a *book*.

FUN MONEY PROFILE

Lori Steffen and Jeff Wark

Net Content Solutions
www.eCorePreneur.com

Previous jobs held:

LORI: Dance and gymnastics instructor, construction laborer, ice cream scooper, truck driver, office manager, but I spent most of my time in the engineering and construction industry. The largest part of my "career" was spent as a project manager, running multimillion dollar commercial mechanical construction projects. When I left to pursue my FUN Money life full-time, I was a senior project manager, which was one step away from VP.

JEFF: I've had lots of "jobs"—scuba diver, saturation diver, heavy equipment operator, mechanic, inspector, machinist, skydiver— now, marketer.

Least favorite thing about working for someone else:

LORI: A job just takes up a lot of time. And they limit when and how much vacation you can take. My mom had her own dance studio and closed it every summer. My father was disabled when I was very young and didn't work. As I was going through school, I thought everybody got summers off. I didn't realize for a long time that some people actually worked year-round.

JEFF: I hated having someone in control of my paycheck and telling me when I can go on vacation.

Favorite thing about working for someone else:

LORI: I really enjoyed running big construction projects. I immensely enjoyed the people I worked with. I enjoyed all the challenges involved. I also enjoyed being on a construction site, instead of in an office, and the projects changed every 6 to 18 months.

JEFF: I'd have to say I have no favorite thing about working for someone else.

Single pivotal moment or thing that helped "make the switch" to pursuing a FUN Money lifestyle:

LORI: I took off one summer for three months, to take my step-daughter cross-country in the motor home, in celebration of her high school graduation. After I came back, I went back to work for the same company. My desire to travel more was high, and my partner, Jeff, wanted to travel more, too. So, we started our FUN Money business on the side. There were changes happening at the company where I worked, too, and these led me to go full-time in the business sooner rather than later.

JEFF: I'd have to say that my partner, Lori, gets the credit for my switch. We both wanted to have a business that would let us travel when we wanted. We were both tried of answering to someone else.

Emotional reactions when making the decision to quit the day job:

LORI: It was exciting and scary, at the same time. I'd been with the same company for 13 years, enjoyed the work, and I had a steady paycheck and benefits. But, things were changing, both with me and with the company, so I went for it with a full level of commitment and excitement.

JEFF: That's easy—*"freedom."* It was like making a sky dive, being free.

Reaction of your friends, family, and loved ones to your decision:

LORI: My friends, family, and loved ones were very supportive. I've always been independent, determined, and hard-headed, so it didn't really surprise them. My coworkers were rather surprised that I actually followed through and did it—they thought I'd change my mind, and I don't think they really wanted to see me leave.

JEFF: It didn't surprise my children. They think I'm nuts, anyway. My mother is very skeptical, still. The rest of the family just watches and makes their comments—some good, some bad. It doesn't matter to me what they think.

Time required to attain the FUN Money lifestyle:

LORI: Isn't a large part of the FUN Money lifestyle freedom? The first weekday I woke up and didn't have to go to a job—that was freedom. That was living the FUN Money lifestyle.

JEFF: When Lori and I started our business, I quit my full-time job in six months. Lori quit her job after one year.

What you do now:

LORI: A large focus of our business is helping people to develop content, quickly and easily. That content can be for their web sites, articles, newsletters, e-books, teleseminars, information products, and many other uses. We offer many products to show people quick and easy ways to develop unique, original content. We also help people and businesses by developing content with and for them as a full-service business. We can help them develop one piece of content or an entire product line and web site. We also continue to work in our niche markets.

JEFF: Being the experts on content creation and repurposing of content for many different uses fills most of our time. We have a few courses that teach how to do quick and easy content creation. Our repurposing course teaches you what to do with the content that you've already created, so you don't have to work as hard. We also offer a full service, where you have a niche and we put it all together for you. It saves you time and money.

Your life today:

LORI: Today, life is filled with lots of travel, both for fun and for business—and a combination of both. We have the opportunity to be a part of some really exciting projects with people and also enjoy networking and developing ideas and products with *fun* and cool marketers who also believe that this should be *fun.*

JEFF: Our life today is very cool. We travel a lot and do what we want, when we want. We also attend and speak at a lot of seminars all over the country. We get to meet and work with some of the coolest people in the marketing community.

Advice for other FUN Money seekers:

LORI: If you don't do anything differently from what you've been doing all your life, your life won't be any different next year, or five years from now.

Make a decision and take action. Decide to join the countless people who enjoy a FUN Money lifestyle and take action to make it happen. Believe you can and don't let anyone—not even yourself—tell you otherwise.

JEFF: Take action and don't let anyone stop you. Make the sacrifices that you need to make to keep going. I'll give you an example of sacrifices. I've been a skydiver for over 30 years. I average about 200 jumps a year. Lori, my partner, has also been skydiving for about 14 years. Skydiving is very much a part of my life. I'm very passionate about it. But, when Lori and I started this business almost three years ago, we had to sacrifice a lot of our skydiving.

Is it something that Lori and I wanted to do? Absolutely not. But, being free from a full-time job seems so much more appealing; it was definitely worth it.

Wrap-Up

- You're going to publish an e-book and an e-zine, the easy, *fast* way:
  - — Your book will establish you as an expert and attract prospects.
  - — Your newsletter will build a rapport with your prospects and provide you with regular opportunities to make offers to them.
- Plan your business so you know where you're going—and where you're at:
  - — Use a calendar.
  - — Decide where you want to be in one year.
  - — Decide where you want to be in two years.
- Divide each goal by 365 and mark each day going *back*.
- Double your goals to stretch your possibilities.
- Stay flexible—it's all going to change, anyway.
- Use 3 × 5 cards or computer software and create a "storyboard," to plan your e-book, e-zine, and any information products you want to create, step by step.
- Develop your persona some more—add details.
- Create a story for your persona or for your business that fits and will resonate with your prospects and customers.
- By all means be yourself—the *real* you.
- Visit forums in your chosen niche or subniche.
- "Lurk" on the forums for a while and take notes.
- Start contributing your own thoughts and information and resources.
- Don't advertise *anything*—yet.

- As you build your reputation, ask forum participants the following questions:
  - What tools or information have you had the hardest time finding?
  - What *one thing* would make your hobby more fun?
  - What's your *biggest* gripe about the suppliers you currently buy from? (No names, please—this isn't a "bash the other guys" session, but a serious fact-finding mission I need help with.)
  - What one thing do you like most about the supplier you currently buy from most often? (Again—no names—this isn't an advertising session, either.)
- Consider using something like Survey Monkey, then invite forum participants to take your survey online.

CHAPTER 4

SCRIPTING THE PILOT

The one advantage of playing with fire. . . is that one never gets singed. It is the people who don't know how to play with it who get burned up.

—Oscar Wilde

Now we're ready to start building your free e-book that will provide you with a pivotal part of my simple three-step formula. I promised you this would be easy. Trust me. It's not only easy, but fun—when you do it the way I'm going to show you.

Even better, the steps you take to create your first book also set things up to make putting together a newsletter or blog simple, too.

I want you to know I do understand your hesitation. *Writing* a book can be a *ton* of work. As I write this, I'm halfway through writing *this* book, and I can tell you, it's a *lot* of work. Fortunately, I love to write, so it's also *fun* work. That's what this entire process is all about.

But, you seriously don't have to write a word. And the benefits— producing your own unique information products and selling them successfully—can actually improve if you *don't* concern yourself with writing anything.

I'll show you the way.

Even if you did have to write a book from scratch, cover-to-cover, I'd still advise you to do it to launch your business because it's so important to success in any field. The power of having written a book is simply too huge to ignore. These days, you're actually working at a serious disadvantage if you *don't* write a book.

People look up to authors. They always have and they always will. Face it—you do, too. And they look up to *publishers* even more.

A SMALL SOCIAL EXPERIMENT

If you don't believe this, try a little experiment the next time you're at the local tavern, attending a cocktail party, or trying desperately to avoid buying more Tupperware at a neighbor's sales party.

Go into the room and quietly observe everyone's reaction to you. Pretty normal, right? Let things go along normally for a bit. Converse normally. Meet and greet everyone you can.

Whenever someone you've met asks, "What do you do?" answer, "I'm a publisher."

I know—it might be a white lie at this point in time. If it makes you feel better, this is research. It's an experiment, and the experiment won't work if you say, "I want to be an publisher" or "I plan to be a publisher." Say this and everyone will politely nod their heads, say something like "oh—uh-huh," and then quickly change the subject.

Say you *are* a publisher, however, and the whole atmosphere will change. The whole attitude of the people you're talking to will instantly shift. You will almost *see* a difference in the way they perceive you in their eyes.

Give everyone enough time to spread the word around the room, and you'll probably find you're the center of attention for the rest of the evening.

If you're vehemently opposed to telling *any* lies (even a harmless white lie that will soon be true anyway), write a letter *about* the book you plan to create. Print it out and mail it to your mom or dad, brother or sister. Write it to a good friend. Post it on a blog somewhere.

Now you've published. Now you *are* a publisher, and you can say so with authority.

Thank God most people don't understand how easy it is to publish a book or their perception might change. You're now going to be privy to this information, but remember—most people will never understand that books are *easy* to put together, if you know how to do it the right way.

Just because you're about to discover a method you can use to, conceivably, create a complete book in two days or less—without writing a word if you don't want to—doesn't mean you won't receive the same instant credibility and expert status any other author gets the moment his or her book is published.

Just don't tell anybody else how easy it is, and we'll both benefit from this little secret, okay? If someone you care deeply about presses you—just tell them to buy this book.

Let's get that book going so you never have to "fib" about being a publisher again.

IF YOU *CAN* WRITE — *GREAT!*

Please don't let all my claims that you don't have to write a word turn you off if you happen to enjoy writing. If you can write, creating books and newsletters will be even easier for you, because I'm about to present some alternatives to writing that you can add to your toolkit and speed up the entire process.

If you can't write or simply want to avoid writing any way possible (and I don't blame you), you can skip this section. You don't need it and it doesn't apply to you, so you'll still be fine if you jump directly to the next section. However—I would encourage you to study the rest of this section, anyway. It could just get you fired up about *learning* to write.

The rest of you (an admittedly small minority) can pat yourselves on the back. You possess a skill that is going to give you a *great* push down the road to turning your passion into FUN Money.

I would first suggest, based on your research so far, that you start writing your "story"—the behind-the-scenes tale that leads prospects and customers up to the current moment. This should include your history with your passion, things you've done that qualify you as knowing things the reader wants to learn, contacts you've made that you can tap to deliver continued education and assistance in their own efforts to follow their passion—and how you met those people and found those resources.

In the same story—or in a second story—tell how you came to the decision to launch your business. Detail in your own words the steps you took to get your business up and rolling. Also write your company's mission statement—what you hope to accomplish through your business–in 100 words or less.

This might sound easy to a writer, but I've found that, generally, writing just 100 words is much harder than writing 10,000. Still, give it a try. Getting your company's mission statement down in 100 words or less, capturing your entire goal, your company's reason for being, in those few words (less than 100, if you can—the fewer the better) is never as easy as it might at first seem. But it will give you a great "hook" you can use throughout the life of your business, so prospects instantly know who they're dealing with and why your business is different.

Publishers — Start Your Engines

Now you're ready to focus on putting your book together.

After you've done the research Jenny's done, drill down to the one thing your prospective customers most want to know about. This will most likely be the book you should put together, addressing that need.

Think about the portions of the book that you could write from your own perspective. Maybe you only plan to comment on other sources you've gathered—you'll feel a lot more like doing this after you've read the rest of my quick book creation method, trust me. Perhaps there are some personal stories you could relate that best show the readers what you know.

Start mapping these out and write them now, if you'd like. Or, wait until we're through the rest of this section.

Next, you should seriously consider studying the fine art of copy writing—creating compelling sales letters and ads that make people want to buy.

If you *love* writing and that's your passion, you could also start thinking about some original articles you could quickly write to get people interested in the book you're going to create.

Writing original articles is a great way to cheaply promote any business. There are literally *hundreds* of article directory sites on the Web where you can upload original articles you've written and give them away to web sites and newsletters that can the publish your article for free.

Just perform a search for "free articles" with your favorite search engine. You'll find more sites offering free downloadable royalty-free articles than there are shoes in most women's closets. A *lot* more!

The power of writing articles lies in the fact that all the authors of these free articles include a resource box at the bottom of each piece they write and give away. The directory sites all state that people can download and use these articles free, but they *must* be used in their entirety, unedited in any way. This means that each web site and newsletter that downloads and publishes your free articles also must publish your resource box—which leads people directly to whatever web site you wish to promote with your article.

You can also write original articles for any of the leading print magazines in your chosen niche. Send them to the editor with a letter telling her that she's free to use your article at no charge. All you ask is that she also includes your resource box at the bottom.

I've used this technique many times. One of my marketing friends has used this technique—with print magazines—to generate literally hundreds of thousands of dollars in sales at no cost.

Make sure you grant print publications "first rights only." This means they can only publish your article once, then all rights to publish the piece revert back to you. Also make sure you only send each article that you write to one print publication at a time.

You *could* make it clear, in your letter, that you're also submitting your article to other publications—but that will usually result in editors never considering it.

In all honesty, this is the most important new skill you could learn to turn your love of writing into a powerful tool for growing any business. If you already know how to create a compelling story and keep readers interested, you should learn to add the power to *influence* people and encourage them to *buy* with your writing— and you'll be unstoppable, capable of generating cash whenever you need it.

Copy writing (sales letters, ads, and web site copy) is a great way to turn your love of writing into a business in its own right.

There are literally *thousands* of businesses—online and offline— that need your ability to persuade people to buy. Good copywriters honestly earn more money per word than any other writers in the world. J. K. Rowling and Stephen King might be exceptions.

Good copywriters regularly command $5,000, $10,000 and more for a single sales letter of 8 to 16 pages. If you're studying and still getting it down, try charging a "discounted" price of $500 for an

8-page letter. This will *still* beat, hands down, the per-word rate most magazines pay for articles.

As copywriters get better and they become "in demand," they also demand (and get) a percentage of the sales that their letters generate.

Think about it. Where else can you find a magazine or book publisher willing to pay *that* kind of money for a few thousand words—with an ongoing stream of revenue on the back end that can bring in tens or even hundreds of thousands of dollars more?

I bring this up because this book is all about turning your passion into FUN Money. If writing is truly your passion, this is one way to turn that passion into cash that most writers never consider. Study the best copywriters in the world today. Look at the letters and ads they've created. Copy them, then develop your own style, and you could be in business for yourself.

Until you've got a few clients under your belt, you might even consider writing a few sales letters or ads for local businesses at no charge whatsoever—except for a percentage of the direct new business that your copy brings in. This will remove *all* risk for them. They'll be more apt to give your copywriting talents a try. After just a few of these, you also should have some strong testimonials about your work that will increase demand for your work—and your prices.

At the very least, take a look into the fine art of writing solid, responsive sales copy. This is the most valuable area where you could apply your writing capabilities and reap rewards that dwarf the usual fiction and nonfiction markets—without ever seeing a rejection slip again.

Me? I write all the time, but I can't say I love it. It's some of the hardest work I do in my business. I avoid work whenever possible, so I usually put it off or try to find some other way to accomplish my goals without writing anything, if I can.

That's where we're headed with the *rest* of this book.

IF YOU CAN'T WRITE OR SIMPLY DON'T WANT TO WRITE — *GREAT!*

If you're one of the vast majority of readers who skipped the last short section when I gave you permission to jump over it, now we're ready to roll, too.

Frankly, you simply don't care about writing, have no demonstrable writing skills, or would rather write as little as possible, and I don't blame you. But, as you skipped over that last section, did you feel like you might be missing out on something? Did you feel—even slightly—like you're back in school, when they used to separate the boys from the girls and lead each gender into a separate room for those "special" educational sessions?

Don't. You really haven't missed anything.

As the few writers among you who read the last section discovered, you do have a great asset at your disposal if you enjoy writing. Apply your writing skills as I outlined in the last section and you'll do great.

But, there is also a potential problem I didn't tell the writers among you—yet.

Thinking like a writer can actually be a *detriment* to putting my system into action. People who love to write tend to insist on writing *too much* and have a harder time pushing the writer inside of themselves to the side. This can actually slow you D-O-W-N big-time. I don't recommend it.

The reason is simple. The key to creating a book in just a few days is to think like a publisher, *not* a writer. I wish it was more complex, more "stunning." But, it's not. Anything you do to overcomplicate it will only muck it up.

Remember—publishers make many times the money most authors could ever hope to make. For every J. K. Rowling and Stephen King, there are *millions* of authors struggling to make enough money to eat.

I consider myself a failed fiction writer. And I still found a way to make millions of dollars writing and publishing in spite of this apparent failure.

I made the decision to *stop* trying to convince nameless, faceless editors to publish my writing for me. Had I continued working at it, I know I would have eventually made it work. I even started a newsletter for science fiction writers—to get into the industry in a better way—years before I started my video games newsletter.

I was unwittingly working my FUN Money formula even then.

Through my newsletter, I got to work with some of the biggest names in the science fiction industry—Robert Bloch, Isaac Asimov, Arthur C. Clarke, James Gunn, Theodore Sturgeon, and Gordon Dickson, to name but a few.

I even published an original short story written just for me by Isaac Asimov, as a limited-edition chapbook.

Despite all this, I soon learned that my biggest heroes in the industry barely made enough money to put food on the table. Only a very few authors in the field made any real money—and then it was only when a book they'd written years earlier was finally optioned for a movie.

Make *no* mistake about it, earning barely enough to eat, doing what you love doing, is *not* my definition of FUN Money. The only word that fits this situation is "struggle." We all have enough of that in our lives. Let's not seek more.

After this revelation had hit me, I switched gears and moved quickly into nonfiction writing. And I made more money than any magazine would pay me by publishing my own nonfiction writing.

THE *KEY* TO FUN MONEY: THINK LIKE A PUBLISHER

This key point is important enough to repeat—again and again. The publishers of other people's writing generally make more money than the people who *do* the writing. They put up the money necessary to publish their works and get them into the marketplace. Sometimes, a book they publish fails to make any money, and they take a loss. But, overall, they get a cut from *all* the books they're publishing—and they can kick out as many books per year as the market can absorb.

An author might only be able to churn out an original new work of fiction every year or two. Writing a quality nonfiction book can take 90 to 120 days or longer.

Isaac Asimov was a notable exception. To this day, he still holds the Guinness world record for the largest number of books written by a single author. He could turn out a sharp, original story in an hour, or write a great popular scientific nonfiction book from the top of his head in a couple of weeks.

The rest of the authors in the field were left trying to find a way to live on the meager advances publishers of that era were willing to pay, realizing they would rarely see anything else because most books—especially science fiction—rarely sold very well. They were lucky if they generated royalties in excess of the advance.

But the publishers of these books still earned a profit on every copy of every book they published, for as long as they continued to sell.

This is why you want to think like a *publisher*, not like a *writer*. Even if you *are* a writer.

It's a different thought process. Stop thinking about writing anything and start thinking about where you can find the information your prospects and customers need and will buy.

Thinking like a writer will stop you in your tracks. Thinking like a publisher will open up entire new vistas of possibilities for you to explore, regardless of what you love doing most, that can easily be turned into FUN Money, faster and easier than you ever thought possible.

Publishers know where to *find* writers and written works to publish. They also know how to put them together in cohesive ways that people want to buy. They don't *write*. Because they don't write, they can kick out as many books as the market will buy.

Or—they can publish magazines and newspapers and newsletters on a regular basis, filled with useful content their readers want to read.

There is no way you're going to accomplish publishing an e-book *and* an electronic newsletter or blog if you plan to write everything yourself. You might get the book done—in a few months. But, then, you'll also need to churn out that newsletter each week, to back up the book.

Your head will *explode* trying to create all this from scratch. That'll make a mess of this book, and you won't even get to finish reading it so—hold onto your head. There's a better way.

Thinking like a publisher enables you to start pulling in as much information from other sources as you can publish or republish. You want to create a solid flow of articles and information coming your way, so you have the ability to pick and choose carefully. This makes it easy to provide the very best of the information you've found to your readers.

Creative Selectivity Makes Publishing Easy

You want to have the ability to be selective. Your job should involve simply sorting through all the information that's coming in each day, pitching everything that isn't of use. Then, you simply file away information that *might* be of use someday and pull out the choicest gems to publish right now.

The more you have to choose from, the better your newsletter, book, and information products will be.

I haven't been into the writer's market for some time now because my focus has been so strongly centered on self-publishing all these years. When I was, the holy grail of all publishers was *Playboy* and *The New Yorker*.

Enough with the jokes. Check out any issue of *Playboy* and you'll discover they really *do* publish fiction and articles. In fact, they publish some of the very *best* fiction and articles in print today. All the "big names" publish there whenever they can. The same goes for *The New Yorker*.

Both of these magazines (along with *Readers Digest, Cosmopolitan,* and a handful of others) publish only the very best because they also pay the highest rates per word in the world for fiction and non-fiction.

When I was writing fiction, it was widely known that you should first submit your stories to *Playboy* or *The New Yorker.* Then you work your way down the list, to the lower-paying markets, as you get rejected at the higher levels. This maximizes your pay for every word you write.

This means the higher-paying publications get to see *everything* first. They don't have more pages to fill than the average magazine (with or without foldouts), but they get to pick and choose from literally thousands more articles and stories to fill those pages every month than their competitors do, because every working writer knows to submit to the highest-paying publications first.

From those, the few articles and stories that they *do* pick are among the best being produced.

Thinking like a publisher involves seeking out the largest number of possible sources of articles and stories for your book, newsletter, and information products that you can. Build the largest possible streams of news and features and people to interview, and you can then relax. Your whole job can now be boiled down to sifting through what you've received, looking for the gold that will occasionally shine through, like a miner panning at a small stream. And you can turn those nuggets into gold.

Thinking like a publisher will also help you start creating additional information products to sell to your customers. It's the kingpin of your new FUN Money lifestyle. And I'm going to show you how easy it is to do. Fortunately, you don't have to pay one red cent for what you publish when you use my simple system—unless you want to.

A Huge, Growing, Insatiable Market Awaits You

Information products are a huge industry. They're the *perfect* products to sell as you build your own FUN Money empire, because they're so easy and inexpensive to create and the markup is tremendous.

Following the steps I'm going to show you soon, you could easily put together a 15-part e-course and deliver it over the Web. Your cost of creation for the course: $0 to $500 (depending on the sources of information that you select). Your cost of printing and delivery: $0.

On the Web, you can easily sell these and have software handle everything for you automatically—right down to reporting who bought what when and how much you've made. Sell just 20 of these automatically, every month, for $47 and you're making $940 per month. Would you be happy with $940 per month in additional income rolling in like clockwork, month after month, while you do whatever else it is you enjoy doing most?

In a little while, I'm going to show you how to create a product exactly like the one I just described, then easily turn it into three or four *additional* products with just a few hours' work, quickly doubling your sales.

Then you can turn it around and do it again.

Just five products like the one I described, selling in very low numbers, can easily generate a $50,000 annual income for years, starting shortly after you've created them and set up the sales machine. I'm going to show you how to build that sales machine and get people coming in and buying from you.

And 20 sales per month is a *very* low, *very* conservative number. What if you had four products and you sold 20 of each at $47 per month and one that "hits a nerve" and starts selling 200 per month? Your income just jumped to $157,920 a year. With only five products, four of which are selling only moderately well and only one that is producing average business for you.

With information publishing, the sky truly is the limit. You can take it as far and as fast as you can go. And even modest success can generate large sums of FUN Money.

Even better—you start making money by focusing on what you love doing most.

The key is knowing who your prospects are. Understanding their inner needs and wants so well that you already know what they want to learn most—and where they want to take their learning next.

This is the power of working in an area where you're already experienced—the things you already love doing most. You *are* your prospects. It's much easier to climb inside their minds and get to know what they want most because all you have to do is shut your eyes and ask yourself what you would most like to know. This is likely what your prospects also want.

Of course—we've also done the simple research required to make certain the area of interest we've chosen and the products we're going to create will be profitable, so the next step is to get some publishable information rolling in.

FINDING THE RIGHT RESOURCES

Now that you're thinking like a publisher, it's time to put on those new eyes and start lining up the resources you need to put together a book, a newsletter (or a blog, or a podcast or . . .) and some information products.

We want to do this *fast*—so you can start building your business and seeing your first FUN Money coming in as soon as possible. Fortunately, the Internet makes finding information you can sell so simple that you can easily build a publishing business without ever leaving home.

Press Releases

I love press releases. The most frightening thing any publisher ever faces (except, possibly, a live pit viper in her office chair) is *blank* pages. Press releases are one of the most powerful secrets available to people who think like publishers. This one secret alone will help you never worry about filling blank pages again.

Major companies hire public relations companies, spending tens or even hundreds of thousands of dollars per month to have them spread the news about what they're up to. One way they accomplish this is by putting news releases into the hands of publishers who will pass them along to their readers. Smaller companies have in-house employees who handle public relations. Sometimes—especially with start-ups—it's the CEO.

When I was publishing *INFO-MAT* (the electronic newsweekly about computers, software, and computer bulletin boards) I relied on

Bacon's Directory to list my publication. *Bacon's* is a directory for public relations people, listing all the different editors and publishers, providing information on how best to reach them.

After a few weeks or months, I'd start receiving press releases from all kinds of computer and software companies.

Today, press releases are sent by e-mail and fax, in addition to through the mail. And they are posted for the public to read on numerous web sites that specialize in press release distribution.

You're free to use press releases in any way you wish, word for word. You can also edit them any way you want. The people who issue press releases *dream* about getting people to publish their releases word for word.

Press releases make great *easy* content you can use to put together books and information products. They're also *perfect* for newsletters (they don't call them *news releases* for nothing).

Public relations firms will also sometimes release white papers. These are incredible resources for publishers. Also free to publish word for word, white papers generally detail case studies or document research results. They can form the basis of entire chapters of books or complete articles in a newsletter.

But, perhaps even more importantly, press releases also always include *contact* information. No one issues a press release without including a phone number and e-mail address where you can reach the person who issued the release. Often, one or more of the people mentioned in the release will also be openly available for interviews.

Valuable Points of Contact

Press releases often include a block of copy at the end that invites the media to contact the company for interviews, sample products, and additional information.

Contact someone involved with the topic of the release and interview her on tape. Then have the interview transcribed. This can easily be edited into a complete free e-book to give away or an information product you can sell.

I don't see much writing required to do this yet, do you?

It used to take forever to get listed in *Bacon's Directory* and start receiving releases. Today, thanks to the Internet, you don't have to wait months, weeks, or even days to start receiving boatloads of releases. There are now *dozens* of large press release distribution sites on the

Web. You can browse them from the comfort of your home, select only the stories you want to use, and start publishing—within a few minutes.

Start with www.PRWeb.com. This *huge* online repository of press releases is ideal for FUN Money seekers just starting out. PRWeb lets you sign up to receive press releases even if you haven't started a publication yet. Just list yourself as a freelancer and you're in. Most of the other press release outlets require that you list any publications that you currently write for, but PRWeb doesn't require that you do.

Signing up as a freelancer will allow you to select topics that are close to the niche or subniche that you cover. This enables you to hone in on just the subjects you know your readers are most interested in learning more about. The PRWeb system then automatically sends you all the press releases that fit the categories you've selected, every day.

You can ask that releases be sent to your e-mail box or subscribe to an RSS feed that will deliver new releases directly to your desktop. I suggest the latter as PRWeb tends to cancel your subscription the moment an e-mail they've sent to you bounces. I found myself constantly going back to my PRWeb account and reselecting "subscribe" to start my feeds up again.

After doing this daily for about two weeks, I succumbed and subscribed to their RSS feed, but you can also simply visit the site and look at all the releases coming in each day. It's actually pretty amazing.

There are several thousand new releases issued on PRWeb every day. The site appears to be growing constantly, too. There should always be plenty of new tidbits on this one site to keep any publisher happy.

I recommend you visit PRWeb. Subscribe to their media feeds, select those categories of news that most closely fit the niche or subniche that you're covering. See how many releases you start receiving each day. If there aren't enough solid stories coming in daily to more than fill a weekly electronic newsletter (three short articles or less can easily be an entire issue), consider changing the topic of your newsletter, broadening the focus a bit.

You can turn one or two really good news items into a complete weekly newsletter. Get additional comments from the contacts listed on each release. Ask them a couple of questions, record your interview, and have it transcribed. It will help fill up your newsletter quickly with information your readers will appreciate receiving.

Again—I didn't see much in that last paragraph about writing anything. This works for *everyone* who learns to think like a publisher.

PRNewswire (www.PRNewswire.com) is another huge press release site you can use. They also let you sign up as media to receive targeted feeds of press releases, but they're a bit touchier about freelancers. They accept freelancers and bloggers, but they do require that you list at least one publication that you've written for—or one web site where something you've written has been published—before they'll accept you and start sending new press releases automatically.

That's okay. Sign up as soon as you get your newsletter or a blog rolling. Meanwhile, you can always visit the PRNewswire web site daily and search on keywords (entered at the home page), pulling up all the releases you want.

Even though you don't qualify to receive releases from PRNewswire, you can still use the site normally, manually searching for news releases. You can still grab the stories you want to publish and the stories that you grab can be used any reasonable way that you see fit.

PRWeb has grown dramatically since it went online a few years ago. They even joined forces recently with Business Wire (PRNewswire's leading competitor before PRWeb came along). Now they're giving PRNewswire a run for their money.

But, PRNewswire is still the "big boy" of press release distribution sites online. You'll see some duplication in the releases distributed by PRWeb on PRNewswire, but you'll also notice that most of the smaller companies use PRWeb while most major corporations tend to gravitate toward PRNewswire.

With these two press release distribution systems at your disposal, there's no reason on earth why you can't easily publish a weekly newsletter that hits the hearts of your readers like William Tell's arrow hit the apple on his son's head.

You could easily put together a book, too.

There are hundreds more press release distribution sites online. Dig as deep as your heart desires. Most of the other distribution sites are tiny by comparison to PRWeb or PRNewswire, but they can still be worth checking out, especially for those rare stories that aren't released anywhere else.

Remember—when you're thinking like a publisher, more is always a good thing. Just type the word "press release" into your favorite search engine and start digging for gold. You won't even get your hands dirty—I promise.

A word of caution: You don't have the right to publish everything you find on the Web as your own. Most of the news and information sources you'll find are copyrighted and can't be used in any way. This is why I've directed you to check out the press release distribution sites. They carry *only* articles and stories created by people who want you to publish them and would appreciate it even more if you publish them word for word. It's up to you to publish them however you see fit.

News web sites such as MSN News, Google News, Yahoo News, and others generally include news items released by wire services that copyright their materials and license these sites to distribute them. That license allows you to *read* those articles but not to republish them.

Stick with press releases whenever possible. There are so many of them being released every day that you'll never have to write a word and still do fine.

Just the Facts, Ma'am

If you have *some* writing skills, and you don't mind editing and rearranging text, there is a way to use copyrighted news items, expanding the available choices for you as a publisher.

I call it my "Dragnet" system.

Just pull the bare-bones facts ("Just the facts, ma'am") out of any copyrighted news story. Write them down. Then rewrite your own story, written around the facts.

This can be delicate if you don't do it exactly the way I've suggested. But it can be effective. You also need to properly rephrase any quotes from copyrighted articles, so that you credit the original source, without violating any copyrights on the news item itself.

I've managed to fill many blank pages in my own newsletters and publications, just by reading the latest issues of computer industry trade journals, taking down "just the facts," and rewriting my own stories. They make great "fillers" in between the press releases and interviews I also ran on a regular basis.

This method takes more work than most of you will be willing to do—but I bring it to your attention so that, again, you can continue expanding your options.

I also use stories in the computer trade journals to track down people to interview. You can do this with copyrighted news items, too. Track down the people in the story and ask them for an interview of your own. Record the interview, transcribe it—and you have your own late-breaking story.

I don't believe this last tip requires any writing, either.

Company Web Sites

When you know your market, because you're already a member of the "clan," you also know which leading companies are players in your arena. Visit these companies' web sites. Look for "press room" or "media room" somewhere on the menus—or just "press" or "media" links on the home page. Most corporate web sites have one or the other.

Here, you'll often find literally every press release the company has ever issued since it first launched—unless, of course, it's a 100+-year-old firm. Then they might cut it off, going "only" 5 or 10 years back.

Either way, online corporate media rooms are treasure troves of articles just waiting for you to pluck and publish.

The contact information, prominently displayed in each of those news releases, can lead you to stunning, original interviews and information no one else has, that you might not be able to get any other way.

Again, when you find a nugget—good relevant people to talk to—record an interview, transcribe it, and you've got material for your own e-book, newsletter, blog, or information products.

Without writing a word.

E-Zines

E-zines are electronic magazines. They're the newsletters that are posted online or sent via e-mail directly to subscribers—just like the one you're going to publish.

Make sure you pronounce the word correctly. I hear people pronounce it "e-zynes" all the time, and that's simply *not* correct. You don't call magazines "magazynes," do you? You're going to publish an e-zine soon, so it's a good idea to know the right way to pronounce it.

This would be a good time to start looking at some e-zines that are already being published. Get familiar with some of the e-zines within your area of interest, and you'll gain an excellent grasp of how to structure your own publication and see what goes into them.

Even better—other e-zines can provide you with excellent content for your own e-books, e-zines, and information products.

You can find sources of e-zines the same way you find press releases. Just visit your favorite search engine and type in "e-zines," "e-zine," and "ezine." Then, try typing in each of those words with the word "directory" after them, that is: "e-zine directory."

Thanks to the vast reach of the Web, there are so many e-zines being published today that there are now entire web sites devoted to the task of trying to track all of them and provide you with a single place to find them. No one directory that I know of tracks them all. It would be a massive task to even try. So—look for all the different directories you can find online and check them out.

Most of the good e-zine directories start out with a list of categories you can choose from. With tens of thousands of e-zines being published, it's a good thing you can narrow your search a bit.

Some directories also allow you to type in keywords and search on them.

You can select literally any subject or niche and find dozens, hundreds, or even thousands of e-zines covering it. Even better, most e-zines are free.

Do some poking around online and identify at least a dozen e-zines in your interest area that you can subscribe to. Sign up and *read* them.

As I said—this will give you some excellent ideas for different ways to format and present your own e-zine when you get going—but we're also looking for additional sources of ready-to-publish information to satisfy the publisher we've unleashed in you, so I want you to also look for writers who appear in these e-zines. Make note of authors of e-zine articles who make sense, write well, and cover their topics knowledgeably.

This is a recruitment process. You're looking for top-quality e-zine authors you can pull into your own publications.

You might notice that most articles appearing in e-zines from outside authors (other than the editor or publisher of the e-zine itself) include a resource box at the bottom. This resource box tells you a bit about the author and, possibly, something the author has to sell. It will also give you contact information, so you can reach the author personally.

Bingo.

When you find an author you'd like to present to your readers, write to her through the contact information in the resource box at the bottom of her article. If there is no resource box, check if it's the editor of the e-zine who wrote it. If not, then look for contact information for the editor or publisher of the e-zine and write to them.

When you write to an e-zine author, tell him you really enjoyed his article, "Insert Title Here," in the "Insert Month of E-Zine Here" issue of "Insert E-Zine Title Here." In fact, you should say you liked it so much you were wondering if he would write an original article for publication in *your* e-zine or e-book, or for inclusion in your information product.

Tell the author you're looking for new, original articles and you're seeking "first rights," meaning you want the exclusive right to publish the article first—then all rights will revert back to the author.

Also offer to include a resource box with the story. In most cases, the author will gladly produce a fresh, original article you can publish before anyone else—for *free*.

Most of the authors you see in the e-zines write for free. They do it to get that valuable resource box at the bottom of each article published, driving readers to their own web sites, where they hope to turn them into customers.

If you must write to the publisher or editor to contact the author, praise her for publishing such a great story. Tell her you would appreciate it if she could provide you with contact information, so you can reach the author directly.

You'll hardly ever need to do this, but you'll rarely be turned down when you ask this way.

Article Directories

There are tens of thousands of people writing articles for e-zines. Many also post their articles in free online article directories. Free article directories are web sites that enable writers to post articles that anyone can download and publish for free. All the publishers have to do is include the resource box at the bottom of each article that they download and publish the articles without editing in any way—and the articles are then free to use any way they wish.

You can find more article directories than anyone would know what to do with by simply typing the words "free articles" or "free articles directory" into your favorite search engine.

There are hundreds of different directories, all loaded with articles you are free to use at will.

Unfortunately, most of the articles posted on these sites are pure unadulterated junk. If you've dabbled with posting articles to these sites, I apologize if I offended you, and I'm sure your articles are the exception to the rule—but it's generally true.

Somewhere along the way, a few people published courses that teach people how to write articles and post them on these directories for free to publicize their online businesses. It appears most of these courses forgot to mention that, to do a business any good, even a free article has to be readable and well written.

Again, this is yet another reason why we don't want to get into the writing business. Publishers have it *much* easier.

If the authors of all these free articles would just read this book, there would be more than enough great, publishable information in the free online article directories to keep any publisher happy forever. But, instead, we need to look through loads of junk to find a few rare gems—people who *can* write well and who also put their articles into the free article directories.

Remember—I said *most* of what's posted on these sites is junk—not *all* of it.

All of the articles posted in free article directories include some sort of resource box at the bottom of each piece. The authors of these articles pray someone like you will pick up their articles and publish them somewhere. They're paid for their writing when you publish an article they've written and include the resource box, telling readers how they can find the author to learn more.

When you find an author you like—don't hesitate to contact her and tell her you'd like to publish her work, but make it clear that you need an *original* article and *first rights*. Be sure to remind her that you'll include her resource box and provide full credit for the piece—and that all rights to the article will revert back to her after you've published the article.

Yes, this is the same method you use to get authors of articles in e-zines to provide you with original, fresh content that you can publish. You'll almost *never* find an author in the free article directories who won't jump at an offer like this.

Remember, authors of free articles write the article first, spending time and energy creating an original piece of nonfiction in the hopes that someone *might* publish it. You're offering to publish a new, original article that they created—for sure.

The result: *free* articles for your newsletter, e-book, and information products, and relationships with good authors who can keep filling up your information products with quality content.

And you don't have to write a single word.

Freelance Writers

This content source will cost you some money. But, if you have a little money to invest in your business, it will add even more great publishable writing to your arsenal.

On any given day, there are literally thousands of hopeful writers wishing someone would step forward and give them a writing assignment for pay. Some earn a full-time living just writing copy for web sites and newsletters like you're going to be publishing. They work from home and charge very little for their work. If you provide them with some steady pay, it doesn't take all that much money to get their attention and get quality publishable material from them.

My favorite place to find any kind of freelance work (writers, Web design, programming, transcription services, graphics, photography—you name it) is www.Elance.com.

Elance enables you to set up an account and post the jobs you need completed, with a description and the maximum price you're willing to pay for the completed task. Then, freelancers bid against one another to get the job.

The secret here is that the freelancers who frequent the site bid *against* each other, so you *never* have to pay the maximum fee you state. It will almost always be lower, with several people to select from, based on their past work and ratings from people who they have worked with before.

Any time you need help with some writing that you can't get done any other way, post a request for bids on Elance and you'll surely find someone who can handle the task for you, at minimal cost.

Want the job completed in record time? Just say these magic words: "Any writer who knows what she's doing can easily crank this out in a few days or less."

This brings ego into the equation. Almost *no* freelancer with experience will admit she isn't capable of meeting your deadline and quality requirements, when faced with this kind of challenge.

Even better—Elance doesn't charge you for listing your requests for bids. And the freelancers pay Elance from the fees they earn.

Elance can be a key secret to your success. You can hire virtually everything you would ever need to set up and run your new online information business, using only Elance—but there are a lot of other similar sites you can explore as well.

You guessed it. Just type "freelance work" or "freelancer" into your favorite search engine and you'll find at least a dozen sites similar to Elance.

CraigsList (www.CraigsList.org) is also a great place to advertise for local help with writing, web design, and other tasks you need for your business. In most locations, it's still free to post ads on this gigantic online classified advertising system, and I've found the response can be much better than a local newspaper. It's definitely better than most of the other online job listing sites.

Your Readers

It might sound a little premature, but your own readers can, eventually, provide you with yet another source to keep your selection of publishable information full to the brim.

As you start building a list of prospects from readers of your e-book and e-zine, start asking them to contribute their own experiences and discoveries, so you can share them with the rest of the readers.

Depending on the niche you've chosen, most people will readily write reviews of products they've purchased, provide tips they've discovered, and submit articles and questions of their own.

Don't want to wait? Launch a blog. Ask visitors to your blog to post their comments for possible publication on the blog and in your other publications, and you'll see some great material coming in that's free for you to use.

We live in an ever-more cocooned society. People *need* contact with other people to feel important, but we're more attached to our computers and cell phones than ever before. Human contact is a dwindling resource, so people tend to turn to other sources to feel they belong. This explains the explosive growth of "Web 2.0" sites such as www.MySpace.com and www.FaceBook.com.

It also explains why so many people take the time to write reader reviews of books and movies that appear in droves on such sites as www.Amazon.com and www.barnesandnoble.com. Everyone longs for his own 15 minutes of fame—and you can get an unlimited flow of fresh, interesting material for your e-book, e-zine, and information products by providing them with an outlet for achieving their goals.

Consider offering a monthly prize for the best tip, review, or article submitted by a reader. If you have a little cash to spare, $100 should be sufficient to shake some great publishable material from your readers. Until your budget allows for prize money, look for freebies you can give away that are of value but that cost you little or nothing to provide.

One of your own information products is probably the best choice here. It costs you nothing to give one away, if it's an entirely digital product. Still, the perceived value is the price you normally charge for it.

While you're still putting your e-book or e-zine together, you can also announce your intentions to start publishing and ask people to submit their tips and articles. You'll get some useable material this way, before you actually launch—but you'll generally find people are much more responsive *after* they've read your e-book or e-zine and see that you're actually publishing what people submit.

The Public Domain

Any previously published work that falls into the public domain is open for you to edit, rearrange, append, or publish as is, as if it were your own—without writing a word.

It used to be easy to determine the exact date that a published work would fall into the public domain. Before January 1, 1978, copyright was generally secured by publishing a work with the proper copyright notice, or by registration of an unpublished work for copyright, through the U.S. Library of Congress.

Under pre-1978 copyright law, a work was copyrighted for 28 years and, during the last year of copyright, it could be renewed for a second 28-year period. That was it. Last shot. After a maximum of two 28-year stints, any work became public domain and open for publishers to do with as they please.

This made determining the copyright status of any published work a simple matter of math. As I write this, it's 2007. Under the pre-1978 law, it's pretty safe to assume any work published prior to 1951 is now in the public domain.

This law created a situation where a lot of great works fell into the public domain. It also allows you to use those works, to create your own e-books, newsletters, and information products.

You might think that anything written prior to 1951 is too old to be of use to anyone today, but you'd be wrong making that assumption.

Napoleon Hill's amazing book, *Think and Grow Rich*, fell into the public domain recently. Originally published in 1937 and later revised by Hill and reissued, the book became an instant best seller during the Depression and it has remained on the best-seller lists ever since.

Wikipedia (www.Wikipedia.com) notes that, as of April of 2007, Napoleon Hill's original *Think and Grow Rich* was *still* riding high at number nine on the *"BusinessWeek* Best-Seller List" for paperback business books—it had been on the aforementioned list for 22 *months*.

Wikipedia, by the way, is an excellent online encyclopedia that's created by the users of the encyclopedia itself. Users submit their own definitions and information, then build on one another's filings, to create a "people's encyclopedia" like none other.

Just take what's posted there with a grain of salt—not everyone who submits knows what they're talking about. Wikipedia is moderated by humans (thank goodness) who eventually will remove or modify erroneous postings—but they're far from perfect.

Still, this is a great example of readers creating the very content that they read. Study it. See if there aren't some ways you could duplicate what they're doing, to involve your own prospects and customers in the creation of products you eventually offer for sale.

Back to *Think and Grow Rich*. The book was written long ago, but it focuses on basic principles that never really go out of style. It's truly "evergreen" in that the principles that are covered in the book will never age or become obsolete, even though the language in which it was written leaves the distinct impression that the words are out of date and some of the attitudes that are expressed in the subtext— especially those regarding women and their place in society and in business—are definitely from another era.

This is why Internet marketing expert Ted Ciuba chose, when this venerable motivational classic fell into the public domain, to completely revise and update Hill's amazing book, complete with Ciuba's own additions, explanations, and side notes. Ted released his revised edition in 2006 and created a new classic edition of *Think and Grow Rich*, written by Ted Ciuba *and* Napoleon Hill, that is his own work, deserving all the attention and profits that have come to Ted as a result—but riding on the back of a solid proven hit.

You can do this, too. There are tens of thousands of books, photos, audios, and film recordings that were created prior to 1951 and you can now use most of them any way you wish.

You can even chop public domain works up and rewrite or revise and update them, use them as articles in your newsletters, create entire e-books out of them, or turn them into your own updated versions that you can sell as information products.

I don't care what niche you've chosen. It makes no difference what you like doing most for fun (unless, of course, your love is new technology or something equally modern). There are tens of thousands of public domain works covering what you love doing from the perspective that prevailed long ago—and this can be a great source of publishable material for you.

A Bit Tougher after 1978

After 1978, your job discerning which works are still copyrighted (and which aren't) gets a *lot* tougher. That's the year that U.S. copyright law was given the most massive renovation it had ever seen.

Today, anything published on or after January 1, 1978, is automatically protected from the moment it is created or published, with or without a proper copyright notice, for the author's entire life *plus* an additional 70 years following the author's death.

Before you attempt to make anything published after 1951 your own, you'll need to do some careful research. The best place to start is the U.S. Library of Congress (www.copyright.gov). They provide a simple search system on this site, to investigate the copyright status of works that have been registered with the copyright office since January 1, 1978.

A new expanded copyright search system was just launching on-line at the copyright office as I write this—but it's yet to be seen how much more accurate or helpful it will be.

I suggest you simply avoid anything published after 1951. This will generally remove the need to spend any time with boring copyright research unless, of course, you've discovered a hidden gem that could provide you with a huge windfall. Then, by all means, do all the research you can before putting your eggs in a basket that could be yanked right out from under you and land you in hot water.

Even better—make sure you work with a copyright attorney before using anything published after 1951.

Our Own Free Copyrighted Material—Ready for Picking

There is one other huge source of public domain materials that warrants discussion here. Anything published by the U.S. government is, by all standards, considered to be also in the public domain.

This includes everything published by the U.S. Government Printing Office or any other federal governmental agency. It also includes any audio or visual recordings produced by any federal government agency, including but not limited to the U.S. Department of the Interior, the U.S. Department of Agriculture and far too many more alphabet soup departments to list here.

This is some *great* stuff—and you don't even have to wait for it to fall into the public domain, because it's already copyrighted in the name of the citizens of the United States—you and me—if you're a U.S. citizen.

If you don't think there's a vast array of information from the government that you can publish, just visit the Federal Consumer Information Center (www.pueblo.gsa.gov/) and take a look around. I just visited this site, and the "publication of the week" was an excellent guide to intelligent retirement planning, complete with color photos, worksheets—everything someone might need to form the basis for a great information product about retirement planning.

You used to have to order all of these great consumer publications and wait for them to arrive in the mail, then scan or retype any information you wanted to republish from them. Fortunately, the Internet age has changed all that. Now, most of the government's consumer publications are available as PDFs, right on the web site.

Instant gratification and *instant* quality information you can publish for free is always a good thing when you're a publisher. This is one of the best uses of our tax dollars that I know of.

And—in case you're wondering whether people will pay you for information they can find themselves for free from the federal government—don't worry. People will *gladly* pay you to find it for them, gather it up, rearrange it, and make it easier for them to get it all in one place.

Matthew Lesko knows this all too well. You know who he is? The wild guy who appears on late-night infomercials wearing a suit covered with question marks (another perfect example of memorable outrageous marketing through creation of a caricature). He's made *millions* of dollars selling his books and courses that show people how to get government grants—federal and state.

Lesko's critics cry that he's doing nothing more than culling information from free federal resources and reprinting it to sell to people—but I'm not entirely certain what the complaint is here. This is a perfectly legitimate way to publish, and people continue to spend money buying the information he compiles and sells.

There are *thousands* of possible niches where you could do the same thing with free federal government information. If selling this information to people bothers you, at least consider this resource when you're putting together your free e-book and newsletter.

If you don't mind writing just a little bit, simply use pieces of federal information and rearrange it, adding your own comments and insights. Then it's truly yours.

PRESELLING THE FALL SEASON

If you're at all still in doubt about exactly what your prospects and readers really want most, here's a system I've used many times with excellent results. It will tap directly into your prospects' minds, enabling them to help direct the creation of your e-books, blogs, newsletters, or information products. It can also put some money in your pocket *before* you've even published a thing.

Or—it might prevent you from wasting time or money creating something that few will buy.

I already covered online surveys and online forums. They're a great way to tap your prospective market and find out what everyone in your chosen niche most wants to buy. I've been using surveys for a long time, and they do work great. But, I've been using them long enough to know that people will also often tell you they want something then, when it comes time to buy it, decide it wasn't so important after all.

This is why experienced marketers know the only votes that really count are votes made with a customer's wallet.

Here's a great way to eliminate *all* risk before creating a product: offer a special "prepublication" sale on your newest information product or e-book. Put up a survey asking people to participate in the creation of your new information product and reward them when they've completed the survey with a chance to buy the information you're compiling at a special prepublication price—at least 50 percent of what you plan to sell it for later.

Make it clear that this is a prepublication price, offered in return for the fact that it will still be several weeks or even a month or two before you can provide the product they've paid for now—that's why the price is so low.

When people fill out the survey, you'll get some great information on the pulse of your potential market. Seeing how many actually order your proposed product can put you in the black *before* you publish anything—or tell you there simply won't be a good market for the information product you had in mind, before you spend any time or money producing it.

Just make sure, if you decide to cancel your project, that you faithfully return the money anyone who did order it paid and you'll be fine. Remember—you'll only cancel if there were just a few orders—so there won't ever be all that many refunds to make.

SELECTING THE RIGHT PRODUCT/PROMOTIONAL MIX

Let's go over our FUN Money formula again.

You're going to put together an e-book and launch an e-zine. The e-book will establish you as an expert in the niche or subniche you've selected (remember the saying, "She wrote the book on it?"—I want that to be *you*) and pull people into your list from e-mails, the search engines and any other promotional work you do.

Most e-zines are sent to readers via e-mail, but a blog can serve as your newsletter just as well. If you use a blog, I recommend that you educate your readers on how to use real simple syndication (RSS) technology to "subscribe" to your blog.

Each avenue has its drawbacks. E-mailed newsletters must always do battle with the spam filters so many e-mail service providers now employ, or your readers won't receive them even though they sub-scribed. For this reason, I highly recommend that you post an e-mailed newsletter on a web site or blog, then e-mail your subscribers with a link and some teasers, urging them to read the latest issue online.

This will keep your e-mail short and simple and friendly with the spam filters.

You should do the same thing with a blog. RSS does this for you, automatically, but few people online still fully understand or embrace RSS.

If you visit www.FUNdamentalYou.com, you'll find a link to some exciting new software I've just developed that will literally make delivery of any blog posts or e-zines you produce a snap—without using e-mail at all.

Another problem I have with blogs is that you generally have no idea *who* is reading a blog. You're not actually building a list of subscribers—they either visit or they don't. One day, someone will resolve these issues. Until then, to help alleviate this problem, ask your blog readers to subscribe to your e-mail notification list, then send them e-mails whenever important new articles and resources have posted to your blog.

You won't ever get all of your blog readers on a list this way—but some is better than none at all.

The goal of the book you'll create should be to impress people with the quality of information you can provide, making them *want* to subscribe to your free newsletter or visit your blog.

Then, you use your free newsletter or blog to continue to reach the people who have subscribed and continue to build a relationship with them that will turn into countless selling opportunities for you.

But—what should you sell?

It's best to decide on an initial product lineup, even if it'll be a while before you can start offering it to your eager readers. Your choices of products could affect the style and format you choose for your initial e-book and e-zine.

I recommend a good mix of several products to begin with. Often, your very best repeat sales will come from customers who have just recently made a purchase. If you don't have more than one thing to sell them, you can lose a *lot* of momentum *and* leave a lot of money on the table while a new customer is "in a buying mood" and filling up an online shopping cart.

A reasonable mix of information products and "hard" products is best. Shoot for finding at least three of each that you can start offering right away, and you won't be waiting long for sales to start coming in.

Information Products

We already discussed information products. The simple work you've already started doing to put together your e-book and e-zine or blog is the same simple work that's required to put together information products.

As I said before, information products are the easiest-to-produce, most profitable products you can sell online. People value the information you sell them—not the method by which it's delivered. Some people will gladly pay you $10,000 for a single sheet of paper—if that sheet of paper contains information detailing all the necessary data to locate and drill a successful oil well, for example.

People don't pay a price for an oil painting that's based on the amount of canvas and paint used by the artist. They pay for the *art* on the canvas.

Put together the *right* information products, and you can easily reap huge, easy profits from sales that cost you nothing to deliver (digitally, online), or much less than the purchase price (for the same information recorded to CDs or DVDs, for example).

As you gather press releases and articles for your e-book, e-zine, or blog, never throw *anything* out that applies and is readable. Label it properly and tuck it away where you can find it again when you might need it. This is all grist for the publisher's mill, and you're a publisher now. Start stowing away information you've found—even if it winds up on the e-book or e-zine and blog "cutting-room floor" for now. Much of this additional material can be turned into other information products that you can sell through your newsletter or on your blog.

Once you start publishing your e-zine or blog, keep an eye out for articles you've published that are particularly well written and informative. Tuck them away, too, filed properly so you can find them by subject when you're putting together information products.

One year of publishing an e-zine, 52 weeks, just one article per week, would more than fill a *large* e-book you could later sell to anyone who just discovered you and likes your newsletter, but who missed the earlier issues.

I just did this very thing with a weekly e-zine of mine, the "E-Wealth Report." This newsletter is made up of one article per week. It helps me build a rapport with new prospects who subscribe.

Recently, I went through two years' worth of back issues of the "E-Wealth Report" and picked out the best articles I'd run, then gathered them into a 257-page e-book that I am now making available to the public.

You can grab a free copy of my new book, "The E-Wealth Collection," by visiting www.FUNdamentalYou.com.

Until such time as you've published your newsletter and/or gathered up enough information "pieces" to put together into new information products, you can also consider selling other people's information products through affiliate programs.

Information Products Have Affiliate Programs, Too

We'll cover affiliate programs in more depth in the very next section. For now, just know that affiliate programs are offered by companies that want your help selling what they've produced. They'll generally provide you with everything you need to make sales, including a web site with sales copy, links you can place on your own web sites, or text to include in a newsletter or to send out in e-mails.

Affiliate programs generally charge nothing for you to sign up, and any sales of their products that you make earn you a commission. Commissions generally run from 5 percent to 75 percent, with the highest commissions being paid for sales of information products.

Joining information product affiliate programs will enable you to offer these products to your customers immediately. You won't have to spend any time putting them together. You won't have to stock them or ship them. The affiliate company does all that for you. They even collect the money and pay you your commissions directly.

I personally know people who do nothing but sell other people's products through affiliate programs and earn a full-time living doing so. One person I know has recorded proof that she generated more than $500,000 in a single year selling nothing but affiliate products.

Amazon (www.Amazon.com) is a perfect example of a huge information product affiliate program you can join. You can sign up right on Amazon, then copy and paste the code they provide to your own web site. Now you can start selling books that are related to your chosen niche or subniche area and earn commissions from Amazon whenever you generate a sale.

ClickBank (www.ClickBank.com) is probably the world's largest collection of affiliate programs—mostly selling information products. Most also pay much higher commissions than Amazon does. Check it out. You'll be amazed at the diversity and quality of information products you can easily start selling immediately through your newsletter or blog, and never worry about creating or stocking anything to make money.

I said a publisher's mindset is all that's required. It's really more like a pack-rat mentality, only this pack rat collects words for publication and products to sell with those words.

"Hard" Goods

My definition of "hard" goods includes anything that you physically ship to the buyer. This can include information products recorded to CDs, DVDs, even printed books. For the sake of our discussion here, we'll look at anything that's *not* an information product that must be delivered physically.

Thanks to the massive growth of eBay and the incredible number of people selling goods on this gigantic online garage sale, it's now easy to find wholesale sources for almost any product you might ever dream of selling to readers of your e-zine or blog.

Here we go, back to the search engines again: Just type "online wholesale supplier" into your favorite search engine, and it'll return a huge assortment of companies willing to sell you products at "wholesale" prices.

I put the word "wholesale" in quotes because I do need to caution you to shop around wisely. There are a lot of companies trying to make a fast buck from people who hope to make money reselling their goods on eBay. Check each company out carefully before committing any money or effort to them.

You want a company willing to "drop ship." You'll pay a higher wholesale price for this service, but this makes it more like an affiliate program. You sell an item and turn in the order, paying a price that's lower than your selling price to the wholesaler. In return, they package and ship the product directly to your buyer for you, without any literature or sign that it didn't come directly from you.

The only other wholesalers you should consider for now are those that will allow you to order very small numbers of each item you wish to sell. Unless, of course, you're in the mood to rent a small warehouse or storage shed of some kind, stock products until they sell, then gather them, wrap them, and ship them yourself.

That's how Jeff Bezos got started in the early days of Amazon, so I'm not about to tell you it won't work. It just doesn't sound exactly like FUN Money to me.

One online wholesaler I know well enough to recommend is Worldwide Brands, Inc. (www.WorldWideBrands.com). They've been around for years. They're huge and have a very favorable rating among seasoned eBay resellers. Their service is excellent. And their wholesale prices and the requirements of their resellers are low enough that you can make a good profit selling almost anything they offer.

And—Worldwide Brands offers just about *everything*. With a total of more than one million products to pick from (everything from tools and cuckoo clocks to electronics and computers), you should be able to find one or two solid shippable products tied to your theme and niche or subniche, to start selling right away.

Another great source of shippable products is affiliate programs. I already discussed one source of excellent affiliate programs offering primarily information products. Here's one where you can find offers to sell almost anything you could imagine and earn generous commissions: www.CJ.com. (The "CJ" in the URL stands for Commission Junction.)

This site offers literally everything you could imagine. Search by categories, drill down to exactly the products you know your readers will want to buy—and you can start pulling in some nice profits right away.

Yes—it's true. You can also type "affiliate program" into your favorite search engine. There should be plenty of individual affiliate programs to pick from—and directories and services like Commission Junction and ClickBank—to fill a giant catalog of trouble-free instant-access profitable products that your readers will be interested in buying, if that's what you want to do.

Go back to the list of web sites you researched as we started our little adventure. See if they have any products to offer through affiliate programs of their own, too. Many online retailers have links to their own affiliate programs right on their web sites. Also note which affiliate products you've spotted that they sell, too. If an affiliate product looks like it would sell well, but you don't see any of your competitors selling it, that could be because they already tried, and it doesn't sell well.

Building a Ready-to-Roll Product Cafeteria

Café Press (www.CafePress.com) is a wonderful resource for the budding information publisher in need of products to sell. This clever company enables you to set up an entire online catalog of hats, T-shirts, coffee mugs, and the like, emblazoned with whatever you want to put on them (photos, artwork, your company logo—that kind of stuff).

These things are all perfect for your corporate caricature.

You can purchase the same items you would sell through Café Press in bulk elsewhere, also imprinted with whatever you want. Each item would be a lot cheaper, too. But, Café Press doesn't require that you order or stock anything. Just put together the artwork and upload it. Then, select the items you want to offer with that artwork imprinted on them—cups, caps, pens, T-shirts—even mouse pads. Put them in your catalog (you can set up your own catalog web site through them), and take the orders. Then, they imprint each item when it's ordered and ship it directly to your customer for you.

You set the price you want to charge. Just set a higher price than what Café Press charges you, and you earn a profit on everything you sell. Café Press runs the order, processes the money, and pays you the difference.

This is a *great* way to get your company caricature or mascot into the hands of your readers and get them to spread the word about your company for you—and they'll eagerly pay you for the privilege.

Start a Club

Membership in a club could be the *perfect* information product to sell to your readers. Remember—people want to feel they belong. It's a natural human tendency. Yet, the Web and technology today has pulled us farther apart than ever.

An online club is exactly what people want. It brings them together with other like-minded people in a system where they can help one another and provide support to each other. This is the "Web 2.0" explosion you've most likely heard all about by now. It's all about people *interacting* with other people online. The walls between web site owners and their visitors have come crashing down, and more and more people want to have their say and participate. This makes membership web sites and clubs, which have been popular for a long time now, more popular than ever before.

They can also build a really nice stream of residual income for you.

There are a number of simple online membership web site systems you can buy inexpensively—or pay a small monthly fee to use. You can then provide your members with new information inside the site. I've included links to a couple of the better, lowest-cost systems on www.FUNdamentalYou.com.

Instead of trying to sell each new information product you create—just plug them into a membership web site as soon as each one is completed. Then, your information products become some of the many benefits members receive by staying onboard with your club.

If you were to charge just $9.97 a month for members to join your online club, and you had just 1,000 members join over a six-month period and stay on board—that's a hefty six-figure annual income. And it's automatic money, coming in month after month, so you never worry about how much you're making. Even better—you only have to make one very low $9.97 sale, then you automatically resell that member every month that she stays in.

It's tried-and-true FUN Money by every definition of the term.

This is like having one of the only real benefits of a job that I know of (steady income) and still getting all the benefits of owning your own business. This could be the entire reason you set up your e-book and e-zine or blog—to drive new people to your membership site, convince them to join and build your monthly recurring income.

Your monthly recurring revenue builds as you make tiny sales that continue to pay you over and over again. N-I-C-E.

Consulting and Coaching

Consulting, also referred to as coaching or mentoring, is more popular and profitable today than ever before. The current atmosphere of widespread approval and acceptance of coaching, consulting and mentoring programs creates a great potential profit generator for you.

Just as you've learned, through this book, that you don't have to be a writer or even necessarily an "expert" to publish your own book, you don't have to be an expert to be a consultant or coach, either.

There's definitely more to coaching and consulting than simply donning a striped suit and shades and learning to blow a whistle. The good news is, there are no required licenses or specialized university degrees required to hang out your shingle, either.

If you know where to look for the answers to questions you know you'll be asked—you can start coaching anyone who has even slightly less experience in your chosen niche than you have.

One of America's most popular advice columnists, Dear Abby, was asked once how she knew the answers to so many questions. She replied that she didn't know the answers to most of the questions her readers asked her—but she had one of the world's best Rolodexes. She knew who to call to *get* the answers to almost any question that might pop up.

I *never* do telephone consulting without my favorite search engine (or two or three) opened up and ready to find any answers I might need.

This is *not* cheating. It's still a skill to know where the right answers are—but, knowing enough about your subject to recognize the answers that you find as correct or false is easy if you're at all familiar with the subject matter. If you can't find an answer right away—simply set up a time when you can get back to your client with the answers to any questions you couldn't answer.

If you're still not comfortable putting yourself in the consultant's chair, consider finding someone who is eminently qualified and who already has a consulting or coaching business set up and running. Establish a joint venture with this coach and generate a solid commission for every one of your clients that you steer her way.

This will help you establish a higher-priced "back-end" product without having to worry about fulfilling on the service yourself.

In the pre-Internet days, consultants depended on a localized face-to-face clientele. You still didn't really need to know everything, but you did have to establish credibility. Usually, this entailed working with several clients at no cost or with a pay-for-performance agreement that costs them nothing until you've helped increase their bottom line.

After you had a few success stories under your belt, then you could start building up your paying clientele.

Worldwide Reach = Infinite Niches

Today, coaches and consultants can utilize the power of the Web to mentor huge groups of people at the same time. This enables them to offer their services at much lower prices and earn unlimited potential income. The lower price point also helps clients make the decision to give you a try, even if you don't have a lot of success stories to share, because they're risking very little to give you a shot.

When you use the online publishing system I'm showing you in this book to market your coaching and consulting business, you've already established your credibility with your e-book and built a rapport with your clients through your newsletter or blog.

Consulting or coaching then becomes a natural progression in the relationship.

In the club scenario that I described earlier, you could offer direct consulting at the highest monthly membership level and work with hundreds of clients paying just $49 or $97 or $197 a month for direct access to your knowledge. At just the midrange price point, that's more than $100,000 per year in income—for those of you reading this without a calculator handy.

Even better—the Internet has had the same effect on this group of entrepreneurial professionals as it's had on most other businesses. Now that consultants, coaches, and mentors can inexpensively reach a worldwide audience, they can superspecialize and offer their advice and guidance on amazingly small subsectors of interest niches and still find plenty of eager clients willing to pay for their services.

As you plan the list of things you wish to sell through your online marketing efforts, consider coaching, consulting, and mentoring at the top end of the scale. You really are an expert at what you love doing most, and experts earn great money.

In the marketing funnel we've been building together throughout this book, coaching fits at the narrower end of the funnel. You'll pull prospects into the widest end with your free e-book. Your free newsletter or blog will narrow the funnel a bit, identifying those prospects who want to get to know you better by reading more. Then, as customers buy more products from you, they move through the narrower parts of the funnel. The higher the price paid and the more often a purchase has been made, the further down the funnel the customer moves.

At the very bottom, narrowest part of the funnel, you'll usually find coaching and consulting. This is also where seminars and workshops, which are pretty much beyond the scope of this book, reside.

Most savvy online marketers will offer two or three levels of coaching, starting with group coaching, like I mentioned earlier—in an online club setting at the lowest available price.

Next comes small-group coaching. Many of us refer to this as masterminding. We offer our clients a chance, at a significantly higher price, to participate in more personalized consulting and mentoring within a much smaller group of people. There might only be five participants or 50. Either way, the size of the group will be limited and much smaller than the less-expensive group option.

I recommend that you consider joining a mastermind-coaching group within the niche of your related subniche. This will give you a better understanding of how they work and what you can do to make yours even more powerful.

Get More Personal for More Money

Finally, there is one-on-one consulting. Here, participants are treated to individual time on the phone with the coach, and the coach or consultant will generally work on each individual client's unique problems one at a time. Again, this comes at a much higher price than for large-group consulting or the narrower, smaller mastermind groups.

I offer one-on-one consulting throughout the various points in my funnel.

At the widest, lowest end of the membership scale, I offer direct access to me via e-mail, 24/7. I will answer any questions sent to me via e-mail, usually within 24 to 48 hours.

At the top level, I offer e-mail access *plus* the ability to make an appointment and talk to me in person, one-on-one, for 30 minutes. I make this available on a first-come, first-serve basis, and only accept appointments during a three-hour period two days a week.

Then there's one-on-one consulting and coaching that I offer to all of my clients. These are 90-minute in-depth sessions that I record and then mail to the client on CD for future reference. I currently charge $1,750 for these.

Notice I said "I currently charge $1,750." I *always* raise my prices whenever I run into a situation where there isn't enough time to work with everyone who wants to avail themselves of my expertise. You *must* do the same, if you're ever going to make *unlimited* money through coaching. There are only so many hours in a day. Even if you charge $1,200 an hour, the way I do, there is still a limit to what you can earn in any given day.

I prefer limitless potential income, so I always raise my prices as soon as I run out of time to work with all of my clients.

This is a great way to build revenue and prestige by going against the grain. Start out pricing your time at a comfortable level for you, to get clients used to consulting with you. Then, increase the rates whenever you see that the waiting list of clients who can't get scheduled to see you is getting too long.

I also use this crafty technique whenever someone calls wanting services that we *can* provide, but that I don't enjoy doing any more. For example, my company used to design and host web sites. During the Internet boom years, web sites were expensive, and we developed a way to turn out quality sites at a really low price, including hosting.

Now, web site design and hosting is a commodity item. Everybody's trying to underprice everyone else. I can make a lot more money designing a web site for my own use, to sell a new product or service, than I can ever make putting one together for someone else. But, I still hate to say "no" whenever anyone calls asking if we still provide the service.

The last time a potential web site design client called, I told my assistant to tell them the price is now $10,000—to start. I didn't have to say "no." The client, in this case, took care of that for me. Had he said he was still interested, *then* he would have had my attention.

Remember, group coaching and consulting can be managed like a health club. Most honest owners of health clubs will tell you they would find themselves in a deep pile of doo-doo if everyone who held a membership decided to show up and make use of the facilities at the same time. But, it simply never happens that way. It's rare that more than 10 percent of health club members use their access privileges more than a couple of times, if at all.

Add a lower-priced coaching option to your list of products and services that you offer, and you can sell many times more slots than are actually available, knowing full well that most of the clients who purchase access won't ever actually use the service.

That's so important that it bears repeating. *Most of the people who purchase your lower-priced coaching options will never use them.*

I once offered a coaching package through a joint venture partner, offering one full year of direct access to me by e-mail 24/7 and by telephone on a special phone number, Thursdays, from 3:00 PM to 5:00 PM central time.

I sold the package for $1,000—and I'll be the first one to admit I started to panic after we sold more than 200 of them. The money was certainly nice—but I wondered how I would *ever* handle all those requests for my time.

My old friend, Russ von Hoelscher (an incredibly talented direct marketer who has been doing this a *lot* longer than I have), comforted me a lot when he told me he rarely has more than one or two out of 10 people actually call in more than once whenever he offers similar packages.

I still had my doubts until I sat by the telephone on the designated days waiting for it to ring. It rang—about four or five times, the first four weeks. Then, it trickled off to once or twice a week. Then, none.

I'm sorry if you bought one of these packages and never used it. The access to me was real. My value as a consultant is without question. Consider the $1,000 you spent, but never made use of, a valuable lesson for the future. And realize that most other people who buy your coaching program won't *use* it fully, either.

The Power of Ten

I put together my E-Publishing Marketing Mastermind to take a maximum of 100 people through a six-month experience, working through the same system I'm showing you in this book. Each person paid $3,997 to participate. I wound up with 75 excellent participants. Together, we worked through the entire process on a series of weekly teleconference calls. In the middle of the process, I held a two-day live workshop for the participants where we could get together, meet each other, and help each other achieve our goals.

The brilliance of setting up a mastermind group is the way all the members help one another. In a group of ten or more people, there are always a few in each group who possess special skills the others don't possess. These can be transferred to the other participants (including you) and enhance the process beyond what you could provide yourself.

I also recorded all the calls and videotaped the workshop, then turned it all into CDs, DVDs, and printed supporting course materials—and sold the course for $997.

Remember what I said about turning everything you create yourself into multiple products and uses? This is a *perfect* way to turn an already-profitable mastermind group into a product you could conceivably sell for many years to come.

I've now completely revised and updated all those recordings, and I've relaunched the original mastermind as The Franklin Guild. This is an online *and* offline club. Each month, Members get four of the CDs or DVDs from the original mastermind and updated, revised supporting materials, plus a live teleseminar call for $97.

It's destined to become one of the largest true mastermind groups ever created. I'm hoping to break a world record with it. And it will help take you through the steps we're taking here, with lots of other people who will gladly help you along the way—including me.

You can find out more (and get a superdiscounted deal if you join, just because you read this book) at www.FUNdamentalYou.com.

Another great way to put coaching and consulting to work for you is coaching certificates. You can create certificates good for a 30-minute or one-hour telephone consultation with you and value them at what you would normally charge for your time, then offer them as bonuses with other purchases. You can also sell them at a discount whenever you want to increase your revenue stream.

Buyers tend to hang onto coaching certificates whenever they get them as bonuses or even when they purchase them outright. Often, they don't have a specific need for the coaching at the time they acquire the certificate, so they hang onto it for when they do have a need.

Most people never get around to putting it to use.

A marketing friend of mine told me a story about how he increased orders on a course he was selling by more than 35 percent, simply by adding a coaching certificate. It went so well, he wanted to test adding *three* certificates to his next offer, to see what would happen. But, he was afraid he might be inundated with requests for his time, beyond what he could accommodate.

After consulting with me (Yes, consultants also seek out other consultants.), I convinced him to give it a shot and to not worry about how many people would use the certificates—it would never be as many as he feared.

He *doubled* his sales and only got a few more calls for consulting per week.

The topic of coaching and consulting warrants an entire book by itself. I suggest you check out a few, starting with some of the books I recommend on my site at www.FUNdamental.You.com.

Seminars, Workshops, and Boot Camps

Seminars, workshops, and boot camps sit at the very narrowest end of the funnel, not necessarily because they are the most expensive items you can sell (though they often are), but because they also require the greatest degree of involvement on the part of your clients and customers.

Public speaking might not have been something you were thinking about when you bought this book, but I can safely say the willingness to stand in front of a group of people and speak (out loud) will easily put tens (and more likely hundreds) of thousands of dollars into your pocket, year-in, year-out.

Seriously—public speaking will come in handy for any online or offline business. There is no better way that I know of to establish *instant* credibility—and it's a skill that comes in handy when you create audio products or when you conduct teleseminars.

Again, this isn't a book about public speaking. I can't possibly cover that topic in the limited space I have here. I learned to speak by taking Dale Carnegie classes. You can also learn from a local Toastmasters organization. I urge you to join one or both.

Consider the fact that most people at a funeral would rather be *in* the coffin than giving the eulogy, and you'll see that speaking in public is one of the most-feared things anyone can be called upon to do.

But—there is *no* reason to fear it, and there is every reason to embrace it.

One Step Above

The moment you step up on stage or in front of a group, you've just elevated yourself above 99 percent of the other people in the room. Instead of fear, you have every reason to puff out your chest and walk up there proudly because, in all honesty, everyone else in the room is instantly in awe of you just because you're willing to speak.

And—it's so much easier than it looks, I urge you to give it a try.

Dale Carnegie classes and Toastmasters will force you to speak in front of the class, get over the nervousness and learn to put your nervousness to work for you. But, you could just try giving a short presentation for the next local group meeting you know about in town. Elks clubs, Moose clubs, and other local organizations are constantly seeking someone willing to speak in front of their groups. Warm up to the opportunity, give a few presentations, and you'll see that public speaking is all about practice. The more you do it, the better you become. The better you become, the more you'll want to do it.

But, like consulting, publishing, and anything else you might want to do to build your online or offline business, you don't even have to speak in public to host a live seminar, workshop, or boot camp.

As you interview experts, creating products and articles for your e-books, newsletters, blogs, and information products, ask your interview subjects if they'd be interested in making a live presentation during a seminar. When you have a dozen or so experts who said "yes,"—book a meeting room at a hotel for two or three days. Then, add tickets to attend the seminar to the other products you're selling through your newsletter or blog.

I would strongly suggest that you act as MC for the event, introducing each of your guest speakers and possibly making one brief presentation yourself—but, one of your guest speakers could also act as MC, so all you have to do is put it together, sell the seats, then sit back and enjoy the seminar with the rest of your attendees.

Each presenter can also be encouraged to offer something for the attendees to buy at the end of their presentations. Offer to make credit card processing available and run the orders, then split all sales with your speakers 50/50.

This can easily turn a $97-per-seat seminar into a $100,000 to $500,000 monster. I don't care how you slice it, that's *always* good money for a single weekend of work.

Workshops and boot camps are usually more intensive than seminars, featuring fewer speakers who each drill down more in-depth on a subject. Seat prices are usually higher for these events, and the number of speakers who have something to sell drops significantly.

Seminar and workshop seats also make incredibly valuable bonuses to give away with a higher-priced course. Any time you offer a complete course for $297 to $997 and up, adding seats to a future seminar or workshop as a bonus works as well or better than consulting certificates—with one major difference.

You must make it clear that you hold the workshops or seminars you're offering as a bonus two or three times per year. If it's a one-time event, it'll lose a lot of its punch because prospects will worry that they can't make it to attend the event on the only date available.

Make it clear that you'll also be offering recordings of the live event available to anyone who can't attend, and it will help elevate the value of the bonus a lot.

Taking Your Sales to Higher Levels

This is still great fun; it's much harder work than the basic system I'm showing you in this book—but it's well worth the effort. You need some good planning and negotiation skills to set up speakers and a meeting space in a hotel. And you have to be able to organize a weekend of training.

I generally avoid working this hard—but I still like to speak at seminars, and I still hold my own seminars and workshops because the money's simply too good to pass up.

For example, let's say you've put together 12 speakers who have agreed to present over a three-day seminar. You offer seats for $497 and sell 100 seats. That's $49,700 in your pocket before you have to deliver anything. *But*—a meeting space in a hotel where you can seat 100 people won't be cheap. Often, you'll spend even more on beverages and snacks for 100 people throughout the day than you spent renting the room.

Most hotels will offer you a free meeting room if you're willing to risk your butt by guaranteeing a room block. This involves telling the hotel that you'll guarantee a set number of rooms that will be rented by your attendees, for a set number of days, in return for the hotel waiving certain fees.

It seems like a really great way to go—but *you* must pay for any room nights not filled by your attendees. If you fail to sell enough seats or if people don't rent enough rooms, you'll find yourself on the hook, paying for every room night you guaranteed, whether there is an attendee sleeping in it or not.

Believe it or not, some attendees will book rooms in other nearby hotels to save money. Others will share rooms for the same reason. Don't ever expect every attendee to result in a room being booked at the event hotel.

At best, this can be nerve-wracking. I recommend you pay for the room and any food and beverages you're going to provide and skip the room block guarantee until you have produced an event or two and know better what to expect.

So—you're going to spend some of that $49,700—about $15,000 to $20,000—on the room and food to accommodate your seminar attendees, with most of that going to food (a pot of coffee really can cost you $25 to $50 from a hotel banquet service, and most hotels will *not* allow you to cater your own event).

Still—$29,000 or so in hand, before you start your event, is good money. And it gets even better.

If each of your presenters brings products to sell from the stage, averaging $100 each, and they each sell an average of 20—that's another $24,000 in overall revenue. Half of that's yours as well—a total of an additional $12,000.

Some presenters won't have anything to sell. Others will come with seminars and workshops and consulting at prices *much* higher than $100. These numbers can get very good. I've made sales of up to $90,000 from one stage presentation (to a room of 200 people). That means I generated $45,000 in profit for my host. And I was only one of a dozen other speakers at that event. Imagine if you had 10 of your 12 speakers do the same thing. It's entirely possible.

If you're brave enough to give a presentation yourself, you also get to sell something—and keep 100 percent of the revenue.

I understand we're talking about FUN Money here—and some of this may not *sound* like fun. Remember—it's entirely *optional*. I'm devoting the time on this here, however, because I realize that some of you, once the publisher inside is unleashed, will naturally want to progress beyond simply creating a part-time revenue to support your most fun activities.

Seminars, workshops, and mentoring and coaching are natural products to move into when you're ready to grow your information publishing business to sky-high profits. That makes them worthy of this discussion.

Spend a bit more money upfront, and you can bring in audio and video recording to the seminars and workshops you produce, capture everything on tape, and turn it all into products that you can then sell for potentially years to come—for $297 to $997. Maybe even more.

This can be a great way to create high-quality information products you wouldn't otherwise ever be able to put together. And you can make a profit while you put the product together.

When I start adding up the kind of revenue that is actually possible from a single live seminar or workshop—I find myself needing a better calculator. The numbers can get that large. This is the biggest reason I can imagine for taking my suggestion that you learn something about public speaking or at least enlist the aid of some other marketing-savvy public speakers and put together some seminars and workshops. Sell them in that narrowest portion of the neck in your marketing funnel as your customers start moving through it.

One at a Time, Please

You don't need to select one of each of the aforementioned products to offer to the prospect funnel we're building together. First, you should only tackle those products you feel most comfortable putting together. Anything else will set you up for failure.

And—for goodness sake—only work on one product at a time.

Depending on the niche or subniche you've chosen to work within, some of the products I've suggested won't apply, some of the pricing examples I've given won't be acceptable to your prospects without adjustment, and some of the product categories will need minor adjustments before they fit in well.

For Jenny, a workshop showing people how to make their own authentic Barbie clothing might work—but she wouldn't get a lot of money for seats. This market isn't accustomed to paying large fees for seats in workshops. She could probably sell a lot of neat Barbie clothes and accessories, and gadgets for making and storing Barbie clothes at the back of the room, though.

Instead, she's planning to produce some of her own training videos, showing people how to do what she does. She'll then sell them on her site as digital downloads and on DVD by mail. She's also planning to add some physical products. She's worked a deal with another producer of high-end Barbie outfits to produce a few items from her original patterns for her to sell.

She's also going to offer some excellent doll storage cases, doll stands, clothing bags, and accessories she found from another company that also offers a lucrative commission split through its affiliate program.

Her high-end item will be, for the time being, her own handcrafted work—complete with a "designer" Strawbarbie Fields label.

Tom would do well to offer direct access to himself for consulting, if he chose to go after the dating market. He's got the moves and lines all down pat, and he could offer a chance for his customers to talk to him personally for direct point-by-point guidance on their specific dating situations.

At the low end, a few good CD sets, detailing his most important steps to success with women, would also sell well and help identify those individuals eager enough to learn more that they'd be willing to pay him a lot more money for one-on-one time.

Albert's a natural for workshops and seminars. His technical expertise with computers and all variety of electronic gizmos, combined with a disarmingly shy demeanor, would make him an excellent stage presenter if he would just go to Dale Carnegie classes or Toastmasters and get over that bit of shyness. He's also well-situated for producing Video Professor-style video tutorials as individual information products, teaching people how to best make use of the latest computer innovations and technological gadgets.

I'm certain some people would gladly pay a monthly fee to have Albert on call whenever they run into a technical difficulty he could help talk them through.

I still need to meet with Gloria to decide how we can turn her love of Corvettes into FUN Money. She's not sure where she's going with her ideas yet—but I know she's ready to get started.

Do *you* have any ideas for Gloria? If you do, you're starting to think the right way. Your mind is starting to lock into the FUN Money zone. It's starting to come naturally now. Good.

FUN MONEY PROFILE

DON STRINZ

Don Strinz Tipi, Inc.
www.Strinztipi.com.

Previous jobs held: I went to school to be a diesel mechanic. After graduating from Southeast Community College as a diesel mechanic, I worked at that for about an hour and a half before I realized I hated being a mechanic. I stayed with it for a little over a year. It was kind of humorous. My father wanted me to go to school to be a toolmaker. The only tools I'd ever seen were a crescent wrench and a screwdriver, and I didn't want to spend my whole life making crescent wrenches and screwdrivers, so I went to be a diesel mechanic. Then, after I found out that I didn't like "mechanic-in'," I went to work for a factory and found out what toolmaking really was. Then, I went to a correspondence school and on-the-job-training and became a toolmaker for 20 years.

I loved every minute of it but, during the time I was doing that, I got involved in my tipi building, and my job at the factory came to a screeching halt, so I moved on to another factory, where I hated working as a toolmaker. When I worked at New Holland—the original job—they gave you a job and walked away, and you figured out how to do it and did it. When I went over to Chief Industries—the new job—there was an unwritten rule that you had to be afraid of your boss, whether you were the janitor or the second in command. You had to be afraid of everybody above you. And they would not tell you what they wanted done. They'd tell you, "I need a hole drilled that big." And then, after you got that hole drilled, they'd say, "Okay, now I need a bolt so big put into it." And it was like, "Wait a minute—why don't you tell me what you want, and I'll just do it?"

I worked night shift. No respect at all, half the money that I was making before. This was in the fall of the year. I told my wife: come spring, we're going out on our own, and I'll make it through the summer. And, if I have to, I'll go back to work—but I'm not going to do it until I have to.

At that time, I was working for Chief Industries, and they made a lot of different things. They started out building steel buildings and went on to making many, many things, and the fellow who owned the place was pretty well noted for "borrowing" other people's patents. That was what he did for a living. He'd gotten hold of a patent—rightfully or wrongfully—called the "Easy Line Frame Straightener." It was designed to straighten the frames on cars that had been in accidents. It was a very, very good machine, but it was terribly expensive, and he'd invested almost everything the company had into getting this thing going. And it wasn't going. One day, one of the executives said, "Well—instead of selling these things to the body shops, lease them to the body shops."

In about 10 years, it went from almost bankrupting the corporation to a new rule being assumed that every car that comes off the assembly line in Detroit has to be designed to fit onto this "Easy Line Frame Straightener." Pretty good turnaround.

I took an idea from that. I've got people who want to buy my tipis—they think—but they don't really know if they want to buy a tipi, because they've never had one, and nobody knows until they've had one whether they really want one. So, I told my wife, we can go out and sell tipis to everybody in Nebraska who wants one. That's gonna' take care of one day's work. Then, what am I going to do the rest of my life? We've got to go out farther than that. And, if we go out away from home, I've either got to carry a bunch of stuff with me and set it up (and, as soon as you set a tent up, it becomes a used tent), or, I can take a book with me and say, "Here's a picture of a tent I make." Or, I can point to somebody else's tent and say, "I make one kind of like that or kind of like that." Or, I can come up with a company named Lease-A-Lodge, which is what I did.

I put out the word that, for a certain number of dollars, I will have a tipi set up waiting for you when you get to your event. You could stay in it for the entire event. When you get ready to go home, I'd tear it down and take it home or, if you decided you liked it, you could take it home and you could apply 100 percent of your rent money toward whatever you rented or anything bigger that you purchased. It was a very good way of making money.

I discontinued that a few years ago, because I got old and I got lazy, and I don't like working that hard. Now, we're kind of reviving it because I've got young people working for me who do want to work that hard.

It's worked out well. I tried to sell the business a few years ago...but my business is more expensive than any young person could afford, and it would take more energy than anybody that's got enough money to buy it would have to to run it. It became a nonsalable item.

Least favorite thing about working for someone else: A lack of ability to be creative in what I do and not having my say in how things are done.

Favorite thing about working for someone else: The paycheck every two weeks.

Single pivotal moment or thing that helped make the switch to pursuing a FUN Money lifestyle: Changing the job and not being happy with my new job. Also, when I was between jobs. I was between jobs for about four days or five days—something like that. And, during that time, I had several of my friends come to me and say, "Oh. I'm so glad you're not working anymore—now we can get a tent when we need it." And I said, "You're crazy. I ain't about to do that." But, then, after going to work for Chief, it didn't take me long to figure out that it might be a good idea to go into tipi making full-time.

Emotional reactions when making the decision to quit the day job: I had a lot of moral support from my family and friends. I do have kind of a cute story regarding finances. When I was working at New Holland—this was back in the 1980s—I was knocking down $40,000 a year, which was really, really big money for that time. And I went from that to being totally in poverty. I even had my kids on free lunches at school . . . it was that bad. I never have taken unemployment or welfare or anything—but I did let the kids have free lunches for a year.

But, before, when I worked at New Holland, I made all my bills and, at the end of the year, I didn't have a damn thing to show for it. Then, after I went on working for poverty wages, I made all my bills and, at the end of the year, I didn't have a damn thing to show for it. I want to know what happened to that other $30,000.

Reaction of your friends, family, and loved ones to your decision: We had a lot of help and moral support from my friends. About five years ago or so, I was sitting at a show we were doing, and there were about four or five of my friends sitting there with me. They said, "Boy, Don, we're just so happy that you made it. None of us were going to give two cents for the fact that you could possibly make a living making tents and tipis." I turned to them and said, "Well, you sons of bitches. You're the same people who sat here exactly 20 years ago, saying, *Don, go for it—you can make it. Quit your job, go.*"

Time required to attain the FUN Money lifestyle: I'd say within three years, anyhow, probably even less than that. The first two years were really bad. But, by the end of the third year, we were doing very well. And then, of course, I outgrew my pants for a while and got in trouble that way. I grew way too fast—went from doing everything myself to hiring and hiring and hiring. Pretty soon, I had enough people working for me that nobody could get anything done without stepping on somebody else. And I couldn't watch what was going out. We started sending garbage out the door. I also found out that we had tents going out the back door, being traded for white powder going up the nose. That sort of thing. So, I cleaned house and basically went back to almost nobody working for me, then slowly worked myself back up again.

When you put out 100 good mousetraps and one that doesn't work—guess which one you hear about?

What you do now: I sit and talk on the telephone and make the rest of my employees wonder why I'm not doing a damn thing anymore. My goal—and I'm getting close to my goal—I wanted to make tents and tipis and go out and sell them until I got to the point where I had enough qualified people at home to make the tents and tipis, and I could just stay out there and sell them. It's pretty close to that.

I still have to do things. I just came in when the phone rang just now, sopping wet, because I've been out taking the liner down out of a tipi. And I just got done selling two tipis, which have to be delivered right away. So, tomorrow morning at 6:00 AM, I and one of my employees are going to go drive an hour away and set up two tipis and load the entire truck, so we can head out for Wyoming on Wednesday morning.

Your life today: I have kind of a strange job here. Living in Nebraska, as you maybe are aware—in the summer time, it gets really hot and humid, and just nobody wants to go out camping at that time. So, in order to make a living, I'm forced to go to the Rocky Mountains, where it's cool and dry, to make a living. Then, in the wintertime, when it's 40 below zero here, nobody wants to go camping, so I'm forced to go to Arizona to make a living. It's a tough job, but somebody's got to do it.

Advice for Other FUN Money Seekers: I'm going to give you my philosophy of life: There is no one more fortunate than a person who makes a living at his or her hobby. And no one is less fortunate than a person who turns his or her hobby into work.

Wrap-Up

- You don't ever have to write to create books and newsletters.
- People are fascinated by authors and publishers.
- Publishing gives you credibility you can get no other way.
- If you like to write—define your business objectives in 100 words or less:
  - Drill down through your survey and forum answers. Find the one thing most prospects most want to know or buy.

— Consider studying copywriting.

— Try writing an article or two about your planned book to submit to the free article directories.

— Write some articles and submit them to print publications in your chosen niche or subniche. Include a resource box and offer them for free.

- Thinking like a publisher is the path to success.
- Start with press releases:

   — Visit PRWeb and other online press release distribution web sites and get on any media lists that you can.

   — Select a topic or topics that are close to your chosen niche or subniche.

   — Tons of releases will now start arriving at your door.

- Look for the person to contact on the release:

   — Either the contact person on the release itself or the person the release is about (information for contacting either will be on the release somewhere).

   — Contacts in press releases make excellent interview subjects.

- Writers—also use the "Dragnet" method . . . "Just the facts, ma'am."
- Copyrighted news stories can also lead you to interview subjects.
- Look for e-zine authors within your niche or subniche that you like:

   — Write to the authors through their resource boxes.

   — Write to the publisher of the e-zine if there is no other way to reach the author.

- Don't forget—freelance writers. Offer just a little pay and watch the quality publishable content flow your way.
- Once you get rolling, your readers can provide even more material.
- Offer prizes—even your information products for free—in return for the best article submissions you can use.
- The public domain is loaded with free information you can publish.

- Almost anything published by the U.S. government is open to use.
- Develop and locate a good mix of information-based and "hard" products to sell in your newsletter.
- Look for wholesalers that deal with small, new companies—especially wholesalers that drop ship.
- Affiliate programs are an excellent source of "instant" products you can sell while creating your own information products.
- Create your own "instant" caricature items through Café Press.
- Membership web sites and clubs make great information products to sell.
- Coaching and consulting are extremely profitable services to sell, too.
- Seminars and workshops can be lucrative—at the high-end of the funnel.
- Tackle one at a time:
  - Pick one good affiliate product.
  - Then, select one product you will be most comfortable creating.
  - Build your e-book to get subscriptions to your newsletter.
  - Launch your newsletter to promote your affiliate product, then your first information product creation.
- Add more products and grow.

CHAPTER 5

THE "PITCH"

Work is either fun or drudgery. It depends on your attitude. I like fun.

—Colleen C. Barrett

SELLING ISN'T HARD WHEN YOU'RE SELLING *YOU*

You're putting together a free e-book, and you're launching a free newsletter or getting a blog online. You've selected some products, and you've created a memorable persona for your business.

You're about ready to roll, but, without marketing, you're also ready to hear a deafening "thud" as your sales hit the floor like that little old lady on the TV commercial who can't get up again.

This is where the rubber meets the road. It's the make-or-break, the main reason most new businesses fail in their first five years or less. There has never been a more mistaken concept, responsible for more business failures, than the ages-old dictum often attributed to Thomas Edison, "Build a better mousetrap, and they will beat a path to your door."

It simply doesn't work that way. Build the best mousetrap in the world, tell no one about it, and it's about as worthwhile as a doorstop.

It might hold your door open, but customers won't be coming through your door to buy it.

There's nothing sadder than a bright, hopeful entrepreneur sitting in his or her office, waiting for the phone to ring . . . all day long. Day after day. Watching the clock and working crossword puzzles.

This won't be you, however. You have a free e-book to give away as a lead generator—the most highly sought-after item on the Web. Put your book together so that it overdelivers, as if you intended to charge $39.95 or more for it. Lay plenty of hints about all the added information the reader will get each week in your free newsletter or on your blog and drive readers to the sign-up form.

This is the ultimate online lead machine.

Still—you need to sell people on your free e-book to capture leads, or all of this will be a wasted exercise in self-deception.

Remember, I said one of the reasons you want to publish a free e-book is that it's the easiest sale you'll ever make. This is true. After all, there's no financial risk involved. The prospect can just read about what's in your book and download it if he or she wishes.

But, the Web is an impatient place. People get online to get information quickly and move on. And they face constant interruptions and invitations to move around constantly while they do. You still need to *sell* your free e-book. You need to attract people to your free e-book offer, then convince visitors that taking the time to download your book and *read* it will be more than worthwhile for them.

You should develop a system that, eventually, provides you with reasonable numbers of prospects that you can count on.

SETTING YOUR MARKETING SYSTEM GOALS

Which marketing system should you use? This will depend a lot on your budget and how much time you have to devote to marketing. First, it can be helpful to at least consider the benchmarks you're shooting for with your marketing efforts.

Realize that you'll need to test the marketplace yourself, to actually determine the numbers I'm using here as an example. I'm providing this example so you can see what you need to plan for as soon as some visitors start coming to your online free e-book landing page.

Let's say you've just tested some free online classified ads, and visitors are starting to hit your landing page. You notice that one visitor, on average, is downloading your free e-book for every 20 visitors to your web site. As you watch during the first few days, you also see that one person subscribes to your newsletter out of every 10 people who download your free e-book. This important information tells you a lot, providing early benchmark numbers.

Now you know you'll want to step up your marketing, to see what you can do to improve your numbers.

Later, if you find that, for example, out of five newsletter sub-scribers, on average, you generate one $49.95 sale, then you know you need 1,000 visitors to generate one $49.95 sale.

This is actually not very good. Put my techniques to use when you create your free e-book, and your numbers should be considerably better.

YOU HAVE TO SELL FREE, TOO

Design your landing page with compelling sales copy, and you can effectively double the response numbers again, quadrupling your re-sponse. If it only takes 10 visitors to nab a free download of your e-book, and all the other numbers remain the same, now you need only 500 visitors to break even on each first sale.

Keep making small adjustments in your marketing efforts, and you'll easily bump this up by 10 percent or 20 percent every month— and your profits will grow exponentially.

Good sales copy is important, even if you're giving away a free e-book, if you want to maximize your response rates.

Remember, too, that a sale of *any* kind moves prospects into the customer category. Now you have someone who is interested in what you have to sell and who has made that first all-important purchase. They've moved into the widest portion of your funnel.

You can make your profit on the *next* sale to each customer who buys for the first time. Usually, these additional sales will come quickly, for increasing amounts of money. And they will be a *lot* easier to make, because you'll be making your offer to someone who is now comfortable with you. More important—they're also already used to *buying* from you.

It might be impossible for you to imagine anyone giving you $5,000 to spend a weekend in your presence right now, but it's entirely possible to get that much or even more from a list of customers who have already made purchases from you of $100 to $500, before you make them a higher-priced offer.

If you've developed a business persona or unique selling position for your company, as I did with Jenny, you already have one of the most powerful sales tool "punches" you can add to your ads and offers—you. This is the one thing no competitor can effectively imitate or match. It's the one thing that will attract qualified prospects and customers to you and hold them to you like glue.

The distinctive caricature that Jenny created with Adobe Photo-Shop is going to help her differentiate her business from any competitors immediately. No one else will have magical help from the strawberry patch, and it won't take Jenny long to make an impression on people's minds that they'll easily remember.

We need to do what it takes to place our company in the readers' minds, then convince them there is something well worth reading within the pages of that e-book. All they need to do is press "download," wait a few moments, and they'll have the information they were seeking. This information will provide them with a lot more than what they were looking for.

HOW TO CREATE A MARKETING CAMPAIGN THAT WILL ATTRACT PROSPECTS

Jenny's putting together a free lead generation e-book about the history of Barbie outfits and the importance of knowing which outfits were authentic and sold with the dolls originally, when it comes to the value of the dolls. She intends to cover which outfits were specifically sold with each of the more important collectible dolls and when they were specifically available. She also wants to include a guide to finding and creating authentic Barbie outfits.

This is where she'll really lay on her "pitch" to sign up for her free newsletter, to stay updated on this topic.

To you and me, this might not seem like scintillating reading. I assure you, Jenny did her research, and she knows her market. This, she has found, is something that a large percentage of the most eager Barbie collectors with money to spend have been looking for.

Now she just needs to create some compelling sales copy for the free download page, while she finishes up the book.

Writing sales copy is one skill you really should learn, if you want true control over your own business. You don't have to—there are plenty of ways to outsource sales copy writing, and I did promise you don't have to write a thing, if you don't want to. But, I hope you can also see that the goal we're aiming for—independence from a 9 to 5 workday with upward limits imposed from the beginning—is important enough to consider adding some new skills to your repertoire as you grow.

Here's the big sales copy tip—the one thing you need to know going in that will carry you a long way: Prospects don't really buy anything they need. They buy what they *want*.

You could argue, reasonably, that toilet paper is something we all need. And we certainly do buy plenty of the stuff throughout any given year. More than I can imagine fitting down that tiny hole in the toilet, and it fails to go down more often than I will ever understand—but that's another story.

Still, when we buy that toilet paper that we've convinced ourselves we need so desperately to live well, we *select* which toilette paper to purchase and drag home based on what we *want*.

Some of us prefer multi-ply sheets. Others go for oversized single-ply. Still more rely on scented papers with patterns. Others prefer built-in ultrasoft "quilted" patterns in the paper itself.

MR. WHIPPLE REALLY KNEW HIS MARKETING

Remember Mr. Whipple? He *never* talked about Charmin's versatility at cleaning up areas of our bodies that we usually prefer not to think about. Instead, he played "cop" and tried to bust all the eager shoppers who couldn't resist pressing a roll of Charmin against their cheeks or giving a roll a quick squeeze to experience its ultrasoft cushiony quality.

I'm not sure what harm these poor shoppers were causing. Surely the Charmin wasn't damaged by merely giving it a squeeze. Still—the message was that this was truly *soft* toilet tissue, so soft that people bought it just to sit it around the house and give it a squeeze whenever they wanted.

They focused on the *benefit* (what people wanted), not the *features* (what they needed). That's exactly what you should do.

While a nice long list of features appeals to the logical thinkers among your prospects, everyone responds best to *emotional* appeals. Ask yourself—what *benefits* will someone gain from reading your free e-book. List them. Don't just list the things your book will show them or teach them—list the way that information will affect the readers' life.

In Jenny's case, her book will help a lot of collectors save money by giving them the ability to spot collectible dolls that are being sold as "original condition," but have outfits that did not come with the originally issued doll, lowering their value considerably. She'll also help her readers preserve authentic outfits, by showing them how to properly store them for the long-term, replacing them with less-valuable modern duplicates for display that match the original clothing in every way.

Of course, her book will also tell readers how they can afford-ably replace their collectible doll's original clothing with detail-oriented quality machined or handcrafted replica outfits.

And she'll stress the sense of pride that collectors experience when their collections are truly authentic in every way possible.

I can't possibly give you a complete guide to writing sales copy within the confines of this single book—but I can tell you how Jenny goes about it. Model her, and you'll be well on your way.

I also provide you with some excellent resources if you decide you like writing copy more than you thought and want to learn more, on the official FUN Money web site at www.FUNdamentalYou.com.

It Starts with a Headline

Online sales copy has to grab the reader's attention quickly. You've only got a few seconds to pull someone in before he moves on to the next web site that's always trying to pull him away.

For this reason, the headline is probably the most important element of online sales copy.

When it comes to that vitally important top-screen Internet real estate, forget fancy logos and contact information—visitors want to know, *immediately,* why they should spend one second longer on your site. Entice them with a headline that makes a strong emotional appeal and you stand a good chance of encouraging them to read the *next* line of copy, usually a subhead.

The subhead should be designed with one goal in mind—to get the reader to move on to the first sentence.

And so it goes—throughout the entire letter. Each sentence should pull the reader forward, and it should all be broken up with frequent subheads. You want to break your sales copy up into small chunks—smaller than you would ordinarily use if you were writing a sales letter that was to be printed and mailed to someone. On the Web, readers don't have nearly as much patience as they do when they're holding something printed in their hands. The average attention span is waning rapidly—even in print—but, on the Web, you should focus on short paragraphs and sentences.

One-sentence paragraphs are fine.

Create subheads you can scatter throughout your copy, one every computer screen or so. Write them so that anyone who is a skimmer can actually pick up the gist of what's in your e-book by merely reading the headline, scanning the subheads, and clicking on the *download* button:

- Bullet lists also make great copy for skimmers. They also satisfy a more detail-oriented reader's need for in-depth information.
- Bullet lists can emphasize *hidden* benefits, such as social acceptance, pride, the appearance of being "in," and so on.
- Bullets are also a great way to list features of your book in one spot after you've hit all the emotional buttons.
- A bullet list of provocative questions that are answered in your book can be a powerful inducement to download it and read it without delay.
- Any long paragraph that you can't figure out how to break up any other way can often be split into bullets.

You get the picture.

Another powerful element in any sales copy is what I call the "curiosity bender." These are headlines, subheads, and bullet points that pique the readers' curiosity to the point that they simply *must* read your book to find the answer to the apparent riddle you've placed before them.

A company called Boardroom, "America's best source of inside information," publishes "Bottom Line," a popular newsletter and series of books and reports. Boardroom is known for their curiosity-bending sales letters that literally *force* you to order their books and newsletters, to find the hidden secrets the many bullet points in their sales letters promise will be revealed.

On their web site, at www.Boardroom.com, you can find a solid sample of their work:

- What Doctors Don't Know about Men's Health *More* ...
- Surprising Tax Advantages in Separately Managed Accounts *More* ...
- The Best Shrinks Are the Most Expensive ... *More* ...
- How to Avoid Tax Traps for Unreasonable Compensation *More* ...
- 12 Ways to Avoid a Car Crash *More* ...
- Money Can Buy Happiness *More* ...

I don't know about you, but I find it hard *not* to click on the "*More* ..." link, to find out what doctors don't know about my health, 12 ways to avoid a car crash, or how money *can* buy happiness. Which one of these bullets presses *your* curiosity button? I'll bet there are at least a couple.

If you can write a list of bullets that relate to your book, like these, your sales letter will see a high percentage of click-thru (people taking your free e-book), and your business will build naturally.

By the way—the "More" button on each of those bullet points should lead to the download page for your e-book.

I always start any copywriting project by creating as many headlines as I can possibly think of. Sometimes, I'll write as many as 25 or 50. All headlines should focus on the main benefit your reader will receive by reading your free e-book. I've been known to come up with 100 to 150 headlines for one letter. The point is to churn them out, creating each as a benefit statement, emotional appeal, or curiosity bender.

This list is extremely helpful, even if you plan to hand the copywriting task off to someone else. It'll provide you with a great list of headlines, subheads, and bullet points that can be worked into your letter. Or it explains the benefits of your e-book to any copywriter that you hire in a way only you could illustrate and provides your copywriter with a lot of powerful ammunition when creating copy that will work well for you. It also lowers the cost of having your copy created by doing some of the legwork for whoever you hire to do the job.

After writing as many headlines as you can (25 minimum, if at all possible), you want to hone in on the best headlines you've created.

Read through the list critically, perhaps to someone else, out loud. Which ones are most powerful and compelling? Which ones don't work? Throw out the bad headlines. Then, go through the list again— until you've gleaned it down to the top 10 or so.

If you can come up with 10 really good, compelling headlines, you've got yourself a great framework on which to build your sales copy. Now you just need to select the very best headline out of the 10. Lead off with this as your main headline at the top of your web page. Next, select the second best headline. This is your first subhead. The remaining eight best headlines will then serve you well as subheads.

You now, effectively, have an outline for your sales letter.

Keep *all* the headlines you "throw out" during this phase of building up your sales copy. These can sometimes be cleaned up, edited, and turned into additional subheads or bullet points.

Here are the top 10 headlines Jenny came up with for her book:

1. What's Your Barbie Collection *Really* Worth? Click here . . .

2. The Lie That's Cheating Barbie Collectors Out of Their Hard-Earned Money. Click here . . .

3. The Secret Scourge That's Destroying the Value of Every Barbie in a Collection. Click here . . .

4. How to Automatically Increase the Value of Every Barbie You Own. Click here . . .

5. Easily Add Valuable "Garage Sale Gems" to Your Barbie Collection for Pennies on the Dollar. Click here . . .

6. The One Thing Barbie Collectors Treasure Most—More Than the Dolls Themselves. Click here . . .

7. A Simple Do-It-Yourself Trick That Can Double the Value of Your Barbie Collection Overnight. Click here . . .

8. One Simple Trick That Will Make All Your Barbies Look Better. Click here . . .

9. Get Top Dollar for Every Barbie You Own with This One Simple Trick. Click here . . .

10. Do This and Your Barbie Collection Will Continue to Retain Its Value—Forever. Click here . . .

If you're a Barbie collector, these headlines have a *lot* of what I call "boardroom appeal." Each headline in the list includes an emotional hot-button benefit for Barbie collectors—and they are each stated in a way that should pique any Barbie collector's curiosity.

This is only *one* of many different copywriting techniques you can learn to use—but I use it here because it's really the one method you can use right away to get the highest percentage of visitors to your landing page to download your book. Boardroom used to use almost nothing but bullets in their printed sales letters. Each bullet was accompanied with the page number where you would find the answer to the question it raised, within the pages of the book being sold.

Follow their lead. If you don't want to write anything at all, provide a freelance outside copywriter with an extensive list of benefit-laden curiosity-twisting headlines. You'll get back sales copy designed to build a list of avid readers for your newsletter the fastest way possible.

You should be able to find someone to write your sales copy very inexpensively for you on Elance.

You can even find people willing to write your entire e-book for you. There are hundreds, if not thousands, of very good ghostwriters and sales copywriters on Elance just waiting to pounce on your request for help with very reasonable bids.

Just remember to ask for samples of their work and, preferably, testimonials from past clients before agreeing to any deals.

Should you hire a professional copywriter? That's up to you. Some of the big-name pros charge as much as $20,000 for a single eight-page sales letter. They also often want a percentage of any sales their letters bring in. I don't recommend you go that deep until your business is rolling in the dough and this level of help will take you to the next level.

For now, try writing some sales copy for yourself or find someone on Elance to do the job. You shouldn't have to pay more than $100 to $500 for a good letter to get you started.

You should be able to get an entire original book written by an Elancer for no more than $500 to $1,000.

A Punch to the Body

We've dealt with the headlines and subheads and the overall structure of your sales letter. Now you need to fill in the blanks, connecting the "dots" between each headline and subhead and bullet list you've put together.

This is where the real writing takes place in your sales copy. If you've decided to hire someone to do this for you, you might be tempted to skip the rest of this section entirely. I recommend you read through this section, whether you plan to write your own copy or not—if nothing else so that you'll know the "magic" you're seeking from any copywriter you might hire when you see it.

First and foremost, if you can write a letter to a friend, you can write sales copy. I'm not saying it will be award-winning copy, or generate the best possible sales. But, you know your own business and products better than anyone you can possibly hire. I believe firmly that your own personal enthusiasm for your business, coupled with a strong desire to share what you have, can create compelling copy that your prospects will read and respond to.

The beauty of sales copy on a web site is that it can always be updated as you think of new ways to express your message. Give it a try yourself, put it online, and if it doesn't convert e-book prospects into downloaders fast enough, you can always hire someone (at much less cost) to revamp what you've written—or try a few revisions yourself.

Each sentence of copy that you write should serve the same purpose as the headline and subhead—to keep pulling the reader along. Never let your reader relax.

Look at it like fishing. When you get a visitor to your site, you've got a nibble. If they start reading, that's a bite. Now you have to reel them into the boat. Every sentence should pull them closer, keeping them on the line, reading, on the way in, always wanting to know more.

Be Like Drew

One of my favorite copywriters of all time is Drew Kaplan. Most marketers point to such legends in the copywriting arena as Ted Nicholas, Gary Halbert, John Carlton, or Bob Bly for their lead. I do, too. These guys, along with some of the greats from the direct mail days, are masters at what they do and we all study the masters to hone our craft.

However, for the beginner just trying her wings, Drew Kaplan stands like a beacon in the night. The words he's written have sold multiple millions of dollars worth of gadgets—and his style is one that's easy for anyone just getting started to master.

You might remember Drew. His company, DAK, started out selling nothing but high-grade blank cassette tapes for audiophiles. Professionals and music purists were his market, and he printed and mailed literally millions of catalogs to sell them his wares, which were very difficult to find anywhere else at the prices he charged.

Then, Drew discovered electronic gadgets. It didn't matter if it was designed for the home or office, if a new gadget plugged into a wall socket or ran on batteries, Drew was fascinated. And he shared that fascination in the copy he would write for each new gadget he'd found, adding gadgets, one by one, to his tape catalog.

Drew wrote his sales copy in a personal style, just like a letter to a good friend. He would describe how he discovered the gadget and tried it out for himself. He would reveal his excitement at what it did for him, uncovering countless benefits, hidden or otherwise, that the reader would see when he or she purchased one of these amazing things.

He would even tell his readers how his daughter got hold of this gadget or that, asked to try it out, then never returned it. Or he would talk about the neighbors who still held several gadgets they'd borrowed.

He would tell his readers he decided to buy a gadget for a friend or family member. He would say why he felt they needed it and how they would most likely put it to use.

Every new product Drew added to his catalog received this same royal treatment. There was never a product I saw in one of his catalogs that wasn't described in a minimum of a half-page of loving prose, all sounding like he was writing to the reader personally.

When Drew discovered the very first automatic home breadmaking machines, all hell broke loose.

I remember reading Drew's first full-page description of this amazing new discovery that made bread automatically, while you were sleeping or at work. He didn't tell you all the features until you were deep within the copy, usually as a bullet list along the side. Instead, he focused on the smell that filled the house when the machine started working its wonders and how that smell made him feel.

Those first machines were far from perfect. They baked a clunky-looking round loaf of bread that, if you didn't use exactly the right ingredients, never baked properly. Still, Drew sold more home bread makers by mail than anyone else through his little blank tape catalog.

And he did it all with those very personal-sounding "letters" that he wrote to his catalog readers.

Eventually, Drew's catalog was *jammed* with electronic gizmos of all kinds. In the last one I saw, there was only a single two-page spread at the back still offering blank cassette tapes.

Drew's moved to the Web now. You can still see examples of his copywriting style on his web site, www.DAK2000.com.

Write like Drew, and you'll never go wrong. Tell your readers why *you're* excited, why *you* would read your book. Give them plenty of benefits they'll get out of the experience, once they've read your book. Hint at the miracles those benefits will work on their lives. Tell them how you discovered what you've written and why it's important to you. Even tell them the problems you went through gathering the information—to solidify in their minds that you've put considerable effort into the information you're about to hand them.

Imagine your best friend as you write. You're telling her why she should download and read your book. You care about her. You wrote the book *for* her.

Don't Close the Door before It's Closed

Finally, it's all about closing the sale. The end of the sales letter. The call to action.

Here, you must tell your readers what you want them to do. You describe, step-by-step, how they can put this information—and all the benefits you've described—into their lives.

This is, without fail, one of the most overlooked parts of any sales letter. Countless copywriters jump right through the close—the most important part of the letter—like they're almost embarrassed to ask for the action. This is a sure sign of an amateur.

Never assume your reader will know what to do next, after you've "sold" him on downloading your book. Point the way to the "Download" button. Lead him through the process and tell him what to expect. If the book will be delivered to his e-mail box, tell him that's what will happen. If he must first provide you with a mailing address, in addition to his e-mail address, tell him he'll need to be prepared to provide it to gain the benefits you've outlined.

Everything you do throughout your sales letter should "telegraph" the close—the call to action, the steps you want your reader to take when he or she reaches the end of the page.

A DRIVING RAIN—OF PROSPECTS, CUSTOMERS, AND CASH

You gain unbelievable marketing power when you create your own free e-book or report. Free information is, without question, the most sought-after item on the Internet today.

The hottest information people are seeking on the Web changes constantly. Paris Hilton's latest escapades, for example, might capture the public's interest for a day or two. Or O.J. might be in trouble again. But even in these cases, people aren't looking for information about Paris or O.J. that they have to *pay* for, are they?

Once you have your free e-book or report finished and ready to deliver, and a sales page in place, designed to *sell* people on actually downloading the book and reading it, your job boils down to telling people where to find the book.

There are so many different ways to drive people to your free e-book download page it would be impossible to cover them within the pages of this book—unless you don't mind building your biceps merely holding the pages open.

Available options include search engine marketing (paid and free), advertising in e-zines, writing e-zine articles, submitting press releases to the press release distribution sites, e-mail marketing, teleconference calls, and online videos and audios.

The number of available options is amazing and, unless you go crazy with them, most are extremely inexpensive and effective.

Within just the past few years, blogs and social networking have burst upon the Internet scene, offering additional free and low-cost marketing solutions that you can tap, to alert people to your free e-book and drive them to your download page.

Here's an admittedly brief set of steps you can take to set up a very effective marketing campaign, to launch your new free e-book and start getting downloads (qualified prospects interested in what you have to sell through your newsletter)—at a cost of no more than $200.

AN EASY MARKETING SYSTEM FOR $200 OR LESS

First, write a press release announcing your book. Press releases are not difficult to write. Just remember press releases are *not* sales letters. Forget everything I told you earlier about writing sales copy when you prepare a news release. That was sales copy for your free e-book's landing page. Most press releases are created to tell journalists about something you're doing, to catch their interest and get them to contact you for more information.

Go to www.PRWeb.com to start receiving tons of free information and resources that you can publish at will. This is the same online press release distribution site that I sent you to earlier. Good news. It works *both ways*. PRWeb will make your releases available to a huge list of real-world journalists, bloggers, and newsletter publishers—*and* to the general public through such systems as Google News, MSN News, and others.

You can also get all the details you need about exactly how a press release should be prepared by visiting PRWeb. It has articles and guides on the subject of creating quality press releases that will take you all the way through the process.

Post a press release announcing the availability of your new free book on PRWeb and include the Web address of your download page, plus contact information, so journalists can contact you.

No journalists may ever call. No matter. I've only had the media call me a couple of times from press releases I've posted on PRWeb. Still, for as little as $80, I've had my releases read by more than 100,000 people.

Even better—your URL in your press release will be seen by the search engines as a "reference" back to your download page, located on a gigantic web site with huge traffic, adding credence to your site and moving you up in the free listings on the search engines as a result, driving even more traffic to your page.

Next—set up a blog. Blogs provide you with a super-easy way to quickly post information on a web site with the click of a button. Just set up your blog using simple step-by-step instructions, then cut-and-paste any information you want to post on your blog, hit the "enter" button, and it appears on your blog.

You can set up a blog to support your e-mailed newsletter or make your blog your newsletter. Just search for "blog software" in your favorite search engine, and you'll find several providers who include hosting. Most are free—but you can avoid the hassle of having some ads on your blog that you don't want there by paying a small fee to providers who charge for the service.

I've also included some excellent sources of blog software, with and without hosting, at www.FUNdamentalYou.com.

The real promotional power here is in the fact that blogs are beloved by search engines. Search engines like the fact that blogs change frequently. Search engines love changing content and rank sites that change their content frequently much higher in their listings, making them more visible to online searchers. This drives free traffic (real-world, live visitors) to your free e-book download page.

Make your blog about the subject of your free e-book or report. Post excerpts from your book. Put updates on the blog, telling visitors new things you've found since you published the book. Update your blog every day or two with new articles and invite visitors to post comments to your posts.

Always, always, always include the URL to your download page in each and every post you place on your blog.

Now you have a blog with changing content, visitors who are interacting with you, and a press release on a number of gigantic sites with tremendous traffic of their own. Both are pointing to your download page, giving it added credence (in the online world, we refer to this as "authority"), and your download page should now start moving ever-higher in the free search engine listings.

When you set up your download page and your blog, make sure you add metatags for the keywords you want to rank highest in your free listings in the search engines.

For example, our friend Jenny set up her download page with the keywords and keyword phrases: Barbie, Barbie collector, Barbie outfits, Barbie outfits for collectors, making Barbie outfits, Barbie outfits for sale, collectible Barbie outfits, doll collector, collectible doll . . . and so on.

Keyword metatags sound esoteric and weird, but they're really just strings of words that you add to the source code of any web site. You can see the keywords that were entered on other sites by visiting those sites with your web browser. This is some additional fun and easy "espionage" you can do while sitting at home in your bathrobe.

While the web page is open, look for an option at the top of your browser to "view source." This is usually an option located under the "view" tab. This will show you the actual source code that makes the web site appear.

Near the top of the source code listing, you'll find "Meta" = statements followed by strings of words and phrases, each separated by a comma. There are metatags for the site's name, description, and keywords. If there are no keywords or phrases following these statements on your own site—make sure you or your webmaster adds some right away. Search engines utilize this information to find the name and description of a site. This is the information the search engine then shows to people when they're searching for that particular information. The keywords tell search engines to show your site in its displayed listings when people enter those words or phrases.

Here's the raw meta source code I just grabbed off of CNN.com's web site:

<meta name = "Description" content = "CNN.com delivers the latest breaking news and information on the latest top stories, weather, business, entertainment, politics, and more. For in-depth coverage, CNN.com provides special reports, video, audio, photo galleries, and interactive guides.">

<meta name = "Keywords" content = "CNN, CNN news, CNN.com, CNN TV, news, news online, breaking news, U.S. news, world news, weather, business, CNN Money, sports, politics, law, technology, entertainment, education, travel, health, special reports, autos, developing story, news video, CNN Intl">

If you're not sure which keywords to use, look at some web sites other companies in your chosen area of interest have posted online. View their source code and study the words and phrases they're using. This will provide you with some great ideas for your own keywords and phrases.

Make sure you add the *same* keywords to your download page *and* to your blog (blogs are web sites with metatags, too). Ask your webmaster or web hosting company for help adding these to your sites if you don't know how to do it yourself.

Look through your sales copy on your e-book download page and, if your keywords aren't already there, see if you can logically add a sentence here and there right in the text, using each keyword you've added to your site's metatags, in the sales copy and on your blog comments. Search engines *love* web sites that use the same keywords listed in their source code metatags in the copy on the sites themselves.

Just don't overdo it. Some people try to trick search engines by loading up pages with their keyword choices, to the point that they aren't even enjoyable for a human to read any more. Search engines will actually penalize you and move your site *down* on their listings if you do this.

We've just touched on what is referred to as search engine optimization (SEO). It's a fairly technical subject, but this is as technical as this discussion goes here. This is only a very rudimentary do-it-yourself discussion, so that you understand what SEO is and how it can help you promote your book and newsletter or blog and start building a customer list you can then make sales to, without spending any money.

There are companies that can help you with your search engine optimization. Still, you'll be surprised to learn that, once you've set things up as I've described, you already have a system in place for catching the attention of the search engines, getting listed in them, and moving up in the listings for the search keywords and phrases you've selected.

After just a few weeks, you should see more and more traffic coming to visit your download page. For free.

Your free e-book is also perfect for social networking online. Just visit the public discussion forums located on sites such as Yahoo, AOL, and MSN—or set up an account on MySpace or FaceBook and start inviting "friends" who are also passionate about your niche interest. Share your knowledge and always, always, include a *brief* plug for your free e-book on the subject you're discussing somewhere in your posts—with the URL to your download page.

Don't "advertise" on forums and the social networks—advise. Then, include a few brief words about your free e-book and the URL to your download page below your name. We call this a signature line and that's usually all you need to capture people's attention who are interested in checking out what else you have to offer. If you're contributing to the conversation and becoming a valued member of an online community, people *will* download your e-book.

You can also select sections of your e-book and turn them into short articles that you submit to article directories on the Web. Include a resource box at the bottom of your article that includes information about your e-book and what people will learn—and the URL to your download page. Post the articles in several of the same article directories I sent you to earlier to find possible authors for your information products.

Again—it's a two-way street. Use it both ways to build a thriving information publishing business.

Article directories make your articles available, for free, to web-masters and e-zine publishers to use as long as they include your resource box. Any time an e-zine, blog, or web site runs your article, your link is included. People who read the article will visit. If the article appears on a web site or blog, that also becomes *another* link back to your download page that will make the search engines even happier.

Finally, search for blogs on subjects related to your chosen niche. The search engines will, once again, help you with this. Jenny searched on all of her chosen keywords and phrases, adding "blog," and found dozens of blogs about Barbies.

Post your comments on the busiest blogs in your niche. Get in-volved in the conversation. Add your tagline to your comments and you'll start moving up the search engines even more, plus people read-ing the blogs will visit your download page, too.

This is free, fun stuff you can do in the evenings while you watch TV or listen to music. It will all drive free traffic to your download page.

If you've got some money to spend, you can also place ads in e-zines. These don't cost a lot, and there are e-zines covering most every subject you can imagine. Look in your favorite search engine for "e-zines" or "e-zine directory" and find some e-zines covering the niche or subniche you're reaching out to.

E-zines have several different advertising options. Usually, your only option is simple text ads—like a classified in the newspaper. These ads usually appear at the top of each issue of an e-zine, also in the middle and at the bottom. Top ads are more expensive and bottom ads are cheap. Many E-zines also offer "solo" ads. These are individual e-mails that are sent out to the entire subscriber list without being in the e-zine itself. These are the most expensive option—but also the most effective.

I hope you've noticed that almost all of the resources you can use to build your information publishing products and marketing vehicles can also be turned the other way around and utilized to promote your e-book, e-zine, blog, and information products. That's the beauty of the Web. This is why, today, information publishing is a more viable option than ever before for starting a business with very little money, from the ground up, and making it pay.

Pay-per-click advertising on the search engines is another option. This is the *other side* of search engine marketing. The *pay* side. Here, you post a brief classified-style ad, then bid against other advertisers for keywords and phrases. When people search on those keywords or phrases, your ad appears in the "sponsored listings" area of the search engine results page. The higher you bid, the higher up on the page your ad appears. Every time someone clicks on your ad and goes to your site—you pay what you bid for the visitor.

This is much more complex than anything I could cover within the confines of this single book. Since pay-per-click advertising will cost you money and mistakes can be expensive, I would advise you to seek out help from a reliable course or pay-per-click specialty service before entering this arena.

The best thing about pay-per-click advertising is that it's *fast*. You can set up an account, post an ad, bid on some keywords, and start seeing traffic in just a couple of days–a week tops.

I've listed a couple of my favorite resources for learning more about pay-per-click advertising on the FUN Money web site (www .FUNdamentalYou.com).

There are many more ways to promote your free E-book through the Web, but not nearly enough room in this book to cover them all. Visit the FUN Money web site (www.FUNdamentalYou.com) for a number of additional resources that I recommend.

VIRTUALLY LOCK OUT ANY POTENTIAL COMPETITORS

This is the way to set up your marketing system that will drive people to your free e-book like crazy—and you will have a *blast* doing it.

Remember the work we did creating your business persona? Your caricature? Work up a full-blown personality or build a brand identity around this, and you'll start creating a personality for your business that creates a bond with your prospects and customers that no one can ever break.

Crazy Eddie became one of the nation's largest regional electronics retailers in the 80s primarily because the owner screamed into the television cameras during his commercials, declaring himself Crazy Eddie and offering "prices that are *insane*."

Even *Saturday Night Live* did parodies of the guy.

The president of Wendy's Hamburgers became a national icon by appearing in his own commercials, personable and humble as can be. Kinko's was named after the company's founder, who sported a huge head of kinky red hair.

Make your ads reflect your chosen image and *stick to it*. Consistent application of a persona will build your caricature into something that some people will identify with. These people will stick to you like glue and follow what you do, if you carry your theme out through your postings on blogs and social networking sites, in your articles in the e-zines, in your e-book and on your web site.

Most of all, make the experience *fun* for your customers. Make it an experience they will remember. The worst thing that can happen is that some people won't like it, and they'll go away. The ones who do stay, however, will get involved themselves (if you let them— something I strongly recommend) and tell others, so they can enjoy the fun, too.

It's all about turning fun into money. One of the best ways to do that is to make it fun for your customers to *spend* money with you.

Think about how you can make buying things from your company fit the persona you've created. Look for ways that you can make the buying experience unique and individualized.

Jenny's considering wrapping all of her packages in strawberry-colored paper and printing follow-up postcards to customers on strawberry-colored stock. Everything, of course, will feature the Strawbarbie Fields caricature she created.

Wherever you see your business touching your prospects and clients, look for ways to build your persona into it. Even in the answering machine message. This will greatly accelerate the process of ingraining that persona into the minds of your customers.

This includes:

- Invoices and order forms
- Mailing labels
- Rubber stamps
- Company checks
- Answering machine messages

There are endless possibilities for branding that don't require millions of dollars or the intervention of high-dollar advertising agencies to be successful. Still, they are as effective, in many cases, as a multimillion-dollar advertising campaign in cementing your chosen company image into the minds of prospects with their first impression.

This is entirely optional, of course. I said so before, and I still mean it now. You don't *have* to do this. But, it will make your business-building much more fun for everyone (including you) *and,* when you do obtain a customer who has paid you for what you sell, you'll be better able to *keep* that customer for months or years as a result, if you do.

Acquiring new customers is the hard part. Selling more things to existing customers is how you build true online wealth. Creating a unique, memorable experience for your prospects and customers is the best way to do this cheaply and reliably.

FUN MONEY PROFILE

RANDY CHARACH

www.RandyCharach.com

Previous jobs held: The short and general answer is that I have never had a real job. At the age of five, my uncle—a Las Vegas magician—taught me my first magic trick. I was instantly hooked. My first magic show was in grade five, at the age of 10. It wasn't a paid gig, though—that didn't come until I was 12 years old. At the age of 12, I placed an ad in the local newspaper: "Have Wand Will Travel" and offered my services as a magician to entertain at kids' birthday parties. My first gig paid $6. Then, I quickly jumped to $8, then $10, up to $25, and then to $50 per show during those first few years.

During the next 27 years, I continued to move up the pay scale, and my last public performance was as a "comedy mentalist" at the Riviera Hotel in Las Vegas. My last private booking was as a "keynote motivational speaker," at my then-standard fee of $10,000 for a one-hour presentation.

To summarize: I've been a self-employed entertainer since 1976, when I was 12 years old. In 1981, after graduating high school, I went full-time as a professional magician, mentalist, and motivational speaker. I continued this profession for the next 20 years until I made a big career change (that I'll tell you about in a moment) in 2001.

For the sake of total accuracy, allow me to fill in a few gaps.

When I was 12 years old, I did apply for the job of being Ronald McDonald, the clown. The advertising agency that handled the

McDonald's account interviewed me and was impressed with my skills as a magician. After explaining that I was too young for the position, they promised me that they would keep me on file and that there might be an opportunity in the future. Nine years later, they gave me a call—and I got that job.

I was contracted on a yearly salary basis to be "Ronald." My contract required me to attend training at Hamburger University, near Chicago, and to be available to appear as "Ronald" up to 100 times per year, when needed. It was a blast that first year and during the additional five years that I renewed my contract; but then it was getting in the way of new and greater opportunities, so that was it for that "job."

I suppose we could include my job as a busboy at a high-end steak house for one summer, when I was 14 years old. It was actually quite fun, too. My fondest memory was buying a 50cc minibike from one of the other guys for $100. That job also led to some powerful opportunities and life lessons from my observations and interactions with other staff and the customers.

And then there was the job of being a car salesman, when I was 19 years old. I lasted three weeks. My success in selling cars did come quicker than most others at the dealership, but it just wasn't "fun."

Finally, between performing in shows, from age 17 to 37, I attended acting school for a full year and owned and operated a talent booking agency and a toy company. All fun stuff, really.

Least favorite thing about working for someone else: Having to show up when the employer said I needed to be there. It was an issue for me from the beginning. It was the final deciding factor for me to leave all "jobs." It just didn't suit my lifestyle.

Even when I was working for myself, which was almost all of the time, there were still restrictions similar to that of third-party employment. I didn't realize this or uncover a way around it until just a few years ago when I made my major career shift. It was this realization that my potential was being restricted that led me to *firing myself* from my businesses and from being an entertainer for hire.

There was simply no *leverage* in that.

While I've always made great amounts of money (I'd made my first million dollars by the time I was 24), there were limits on how much I could possibly make. If I didn't want to actually commit to showing up somewhere and "performing" or being around to run my businesses, then the income would disappear and there was no fun or magic in that.

I had created a job for myself—and my boss was a slave-driving nut job—me! My self-imposed superstrict work ethic and demanding schedule was, at times, quite taxing. Not that this won't happen when others employ you—it's just that I knew there must be a better way.

The better way that I discovered is to create systems that makes you money while not depending on you to personally be there—or anywhere—on a regular basis in order to keep making that money. To truly escape employment, you need a system that will make money for you without upside limits or based on your personal calendar or resources. It's the creation and use of these systems that I use now, to provide me with the greatest freedom available, to live the life I want and have always dreamed of.

Favorite thing about working for someone else: Knowing that I would receive steady and predictable money by way of a paycheck was a nice thought. I did appreciate it with my Ronald job because it was a good amount, at the time, and I was still free to do whatever I wanted when I wasn't needed to appear as Ronald.

Eventually, though, my other activities were much more fun and lucrative than the requirement to be available as Ronald, and it conflicted with my higher priorities—so it was time to leave.

Single pivotal moment or thing that helped make the switch to pursuing a FUN Money lifestyle: That moment actually happened during my brief stint as a car salesman. It was at the morning sales meeting, and I'd just been praised by the sales manager for selling his demo car on my first day at work, three weeks earlier. It came to my attention that the meeting for the following week fell on my day off. I was told that I needed to attend the meeting, regardless of the fact that I was not working that day. I said that I would never be attending meetings on my day off.

That was it for that job. They didn't agree with me and insisted I show up on my day off, so I quit on the spot. Of course, I would have left soon enough anyway, but that was a turning point in my mind. At that moment, I decided to become independently wealthy and to have complete control of my own schedule just as soon as possible. I achieved that goal shortly thereafter, through the income earned as an entertainer and business owner.

Emotional reactions when making the decision to quit the day job: It was definitely a feeling of empowerment. It was nice to know that I'd reached a point in my life where I didn't owe it to anyone to be anywhere and do anything at a specific time on an ongoing basis.

Of course, I still had commitments to keep as a businessperson. During the course of 20 years and 5,000 appearances as an entertainer and speaker, I never missed or was late for a single engagement. Other businesses that I developed and built were also run with strict standards that were admittedly personally inflicted. It was me in control now. If I didn't want to commit to a booking date or if I didn't want to do business with a particular client, then I didn't. There's been no looking back and never will be.

Reaction of your friends, family, and loved ones to your decision: It was expected from the beginning.

Time required to attain the FUN Money lifestyle: Even my little stints in the restaurant and the car dealership were fun and interesting. I don't regret those experiences at all. The Ronald job was really treated more as if it were an independent contract, although I was on salary—and it was a lot of fun, too. I guess I'm having trouble answering this one, as my experience has been atypical.

A summer job when I was 14 years old, a few weeks in a restaurant, and three weeks as a car salesman is the sum total of my lifetime "employment" experience. If we count the Ronald contract, it still doesn't add up to (I'll invent a word here) an "Un-FUN" Money lifestyle. I mean—what could be more fun than dressing up like a world-famous clown and making kids happy for an hour?

It was in 2001 when I "traded in my rabbit for a mouse" and started an Internet marketing company. More recently, I tried my hand at producing movies and plan on producing many more. It's here, in these ventures that I have found the ultimate leverage.

So, I suppose the decision was made at birth. Although I leaned into the conventional "work" world for a few brief moments, clearly, I've not been designed to conform to other people's demands. For this, I'm eternally grateful.

What you do now: Same as before—whatever I want, when I want. My business activities are twofold. In addition to my involvement in the world of Internet marketing, I'm also a film producer. I've always loved movies and am passionate about filmmaking. You can find out which movies I've produced by searching under my name at.

Joint venturing with other creative marketers and offering my help as a marketing director for Internet-based companies occupies much of my work time. Everything I do now is based on a system of standards that suit my overall life objectives for my family. For example, in order for me to join a project, it must be something that will also benefit a large group of other people. There must be unlimited upside earning potential. And, of course (and of utmost importance), the project has to be *fun*.

Your life today: I enjoy a relaxed lifestyle now, more so than ever before. As a father of four daughters, it's nice to be able to spend as much time as I want with my family.

My weekday starts around 7 AM, and the first couple of hours are devoted to playing with the kids and/or taking them to school. From 9 AM until noon is when I typically "work." This involves activities such as writing this contribution to a friend's book, other business-related writing, reading movie scripts, corresponding with joint venture partners, and generally making sure all my commitments are being met and that my business life is in good order. That's it for work for the day—and it often takes only an hour or two.

My afternoon always consists of an hour of exercise, either at the gym with a personal trainer, hot yoga, at my country club in the swimming pool or tennis court, or out riding my bike. Often, I'll spend time with my kids after they finish school.

My meals are always healthy and usually shared with my family and friends. I also enjoy regular massages, meditating, and reading. Each day is a balance of physical, emotional, and spiritual activity. This keeps me well-grounded and clear headed, so my "work time" is effective to the point where I accomplish, in my two hours of work, much more than many people (including myself in the past) achieve from working all day.

The key to the success in all areas of my life lies in the balance that I have purposely designed and maintain.

Advice for other FUN Money seekers: It's a cliché, but it's the way I've lived my life, so it's what I truly believe—and that is to do what you're passionate about. Typically, the money will follow, as it always has for me. If the money doesn't follow, then my advice is to adapt that passion into at least one activity that provides you with enough money to live the life you want. While creating income from your passion, be sure to create your business with systems in mind. Focus more on working "on" your business, rather than "in" it. Take moments to reflect on the "why" you're seeking money in the first place and don't ever lose sight of that vision.

Wrap-Up

- Your e-book is a *killer* lead generation machine:
  - It's the perfect first product at the best possible price—free.
  - It's the easiest sale you can make, and it will build you an essential list of e-zine subscribers or blog visitors that you can sell to.
  - Your e-book will build e-zine or blog readership for you.
  - You still need to *sell* the e-book.
- Plan your marketing steps based on projected sales.
- People buy what they *want*—*not* what they need.
- Focus on the benefits your readers will obtain by reading your free e-book.
- Breaking even or even losing money on the first sale is not bad—if you have more to sell new customers right away.
- Small adjustments, over time, increase your averages dramatically.
- Writing headlines—*lots* of headlines—will build a sales letter quickly.
- Headlines, subheads, and bullet lists pull readers through your sales copy.
- Bend the readers' curiosity, forcing them to read more.
- Boil it all down to 10 headlines or so:
  - These become your main headlines and subheads.
  - Even the "clunkers" are potential strong bullet points.
- Your headline, subheads, and bullets, ordered properly, form a sales letter outline you can easily build out.

- A list of headlines, subheads, and bullets will also work as a great outline to hand off to someone else—if you're not writing your own sales copy.
- Ghostwriters can do it *all* for you—sales copy, newsletter articles, and even your entire e-book and information products, if you wish.
- Fill in the blanks, and you can write it all yourself.
- Write like Drew Kaplan, and you'll never go wrong.
- Don't fear the "close"—work up to it and *ask for the sale.*
- Never assume your prospects and customers know what to do next—tell them what to do every step of the way.
- Get your marketing system in place and all you have to do is drive people to the book through:
  — Search engine marketing (paid and free).
  — Advertising in e-zines.
  — Writing e-zine articles.
  — Submitting press releases to the press release distribution sites.
  — E-mail marketing.
  — Teleconference calls.
  — Online videos and audios.
  — Blogs.
  — Social networking sites.
  — Forums.
  — A simple $0 to $200 marketing system.
  — PRWeb—announce your new book.
  — Set up a blog to support your book.
  — Add the same keywords to your blog and to your e-book download page.
  — See if you can logically work some of the keywords you've placed on your blog and e-book download page into the sales copy on your e-book download page.
  — Get on related social networking sites, forums, and blogs and participate—a simple note to download your free book in your signature line does the trick.

- — Create articles from sections of your free e-book and up-load them to article directories, including your free e-book download web site's URL in your resource box.
- Got some money to spend on marketing?
  - — Consider advertising in e-zines.
  - — Carefully, slowly, test pay-per-click ads on search engines.
- Utilize your company caricature in all the above marketing and it will work even better.

CHAPTER 6

THE PAYDAY THAT NEVER ENDS

When you have confidence, you can have a lot of fun. And when you have fun, you can do amazing things.

—Anonymous

RECYCLING: IT'S NOT JUST FOR ALUMINUM CANS

Now you've identified your *true* passion. You've certified that it's a profitable arena where people are spending money. You've created an e-book to give away. You've created a persona to build your business around. You've got a nice sales page where people can download your book. You've set up a marketing system to get people visiting. And you have a newsletter or blog set up and ready to roll or already updating regularly.

Next, you simply recycle what you've done.

Remember—it's always easier to sell *more* things to *existing* customers than it ever is to attract *new* customers. Similarly, it's much easier to transform a single piece of information that you've put together into many more products and marketing tools.

We touched on this when I suggested that you go through the book you've created and find small sections of it that can be turned into articles. These articles can be used for marketing, as I pointed out, by submitting them to e-zines and online article directories. They can even be submitted to print magazines that serve your chosen niche.

You can also turn them into articles for your newsletter.

Likewise, you can turn any copy you've written for products you've chosen to create or resell into articles. Run them in your newsletter, build some of them into comments on blogs, incorporate them into press releases—and so much more. It's easier than you think when you put your mind to it—and it's a far sight better than starting from scratch every time you want to create some new information.

Isaac Asimov — Master Recycler

When I asked Isaac Asimov to write a short story for me to publish as a limited-edition chapbook back in 1978, I never expected him to say yes. He was, after all, one of America's most prominent science fact and science fiction authors. He wrote for all the leading magazines, including the *New Yorker, Saturday Evening Post,* and *Playboy*. I was only offering $200 plus a small percentage of the potential profit.

When he agreed, he told me the payment I was offering was fine. After all—this was a man who could knock out a world-class short story in half an hour. But—he also told me he knew it would be reprinted, after the one-year exclusive "first rights" I was asking for, in an issue of his *Isaac Asimov's Science Fiction Magazine*. And, he always bundled up every short story he wrote and included each of them in his *OPUS* collections, which were released in hardback every time he'd published 100 new books. The story he wrote for me also appeared in his *Opus 200*.

The point is, Isaac Asimov *reused* everything he wrote many different ways. You should, too.

HOW TO REPURPOSE EVERYTHING YOU DO

Repurposing content is the easy way to create one piece of information, then turn it into a broad variety of products and uses. Like what Isaac Asimov did.

A good marketing friend of mine repurposes *everything* he does. He reuses all of the information products he creates, but he also reuses even the sales letters he writes to sell those products.

He told me, when he writes a sales letter, he first looks back through his entire collection of past letters that he's written. Then, he picks one that most closely fits the product he wants to sell next and revises it to fit the new product. This makes it easy to quickly turn out a new sales letter for his *next* product.

As he explained to me, if a letter worked well for one product, why wouldn't it work again for another similar product?

Considering the fact that he's generated more than $100 million in sales with his information products, I think his methods are worth studying, don't you?

I'm now working with two marvelous, talented people—Jeff Wark and Lori Steffen—on a project that could be extremely important to your future as an online information publisher. Full details are on the FUN Money web site at www.FUNdamentalYou.com. Jeff and Lori are *masters* of repurposing content.

Known online as "The Dynamic Duo of Content," they've devised a course that shows you how to easily take any single information product and repurpose it more than 200 ways. They've even developed a chart that makes plotting out all the possible variations a simple connect-the-dots process.

That's why I've chosen to work with them—plus a few other reasons. You can do this, too. And it's easy. Jeff is now a respected online information publisher—and he's a dyslexic high school dropout.

Don't tell me you can't do this.

For example—take the e-book you've put together. Want to quickly add a new product to sell to subscribers of your newsletter? Get a digital recorder or connect a microphone to your computer, so it will record a digital audio file. Then, *read* your e-book into the microphone.

With a little practice, this can be a quick, easy way to generate a CD that you can offer to people. CDs carry a much higher perceived value than e-books. Some people prefer listening to reading any day. If this wasn't true, there wouldn't be entire racks of "books on CD" at your local bookstore.

Offer customers the option, when they choose to download your free e-book, to buy your CD at the same time for a one-time low price of just $14.97 (usually $24.97).

Whether they order or not, take them directly to the download link, so they can get the free e-book they came for. Those who buy your CD will appreciate being able to look over the book while they anxiously await the CD they ordered, so they can listen to it anywhere.

CDs are so easy to create these days it's no problem turning out something worth selling to other people. You can even do it yourself on most personal computers with a CD burner built in (most computers come with CD burners or DVD burners these days). All you have to do is save the file you create with your mike to the CD as an *audio* CD, and it will play in CD players.

You're now done.

Just burn a few copies and mail them to people who order. When you get a *lot* of people ordering, you can then easily hand it off to a fulfillment company who will make additional copies and ship them on demand to your customers when they order.

You can do the same thing with Camtasia. This is software that enables you to capture whatever is happening on a computer screen as video, including voiceover narration. Read through your book into a microphone while running Camtasia to capture a PowerPoint slide presentation on your PC, and you'll also turn your e-book into a DVD that sells for even more than an audio-only CD.

I've listed a couple of recommended CD and DVD fulfillment companies on the official FUN Money web site at www.FUNdamentalYou .com. You'll find the information for buying Camtasia software—and a couple of alternatives—there as well.

YOUR NEWSLETTER—THE CONSTANT MARKETER

Everything you do to create information products will also generate tons of material that you can easily pour into a newsletter or post as comments on a blog. Any one of the resources I've provided here can also be a source of constant new material to bring to your readers—and you don't have to write a word.

The e-book helps you easily build a list of prospects. Your newsletter or blog continues to reach out to those prospects, maintaining and building your relationship while you also offer the things you intend to sell. It works so consistently, you'll see results if you just follow the steps involved in setting it all up.

The first couple of paragraphs of most relevant news releases make excellent newsletter articles. Get on the press release distribution sites and you can easily fill your newsletter with lots of "meat" with this one resource.

Apply the Drew Kaplan approach to any new products you want to introduce to your readers and this, too, can provide you with articles to include.

You could also track down important people involved with any affiliate products you've decided to sell, interview them and include the interviews in your newsletter. This can literally make your products "come to life" in the eyes of your readers, bringing them insider details they would not otherwise know in your newsletter that drives them to buy.

You can create your newsletter as simple text and send it out as an e-mail. A better approach these days is to send out an e-mail to your list when each new issue is released, giving readers some compelling headlines and reasons to click a link to read the entire issue on a web site online.

This works great with blogs, too.

Remember—as I write this, I've just completed development of a wonderful new software utility that will get your e-mailed newsletters and blog updates delivered to your readers, reliably, without using e-mail. I've put more information about this unique low-cost e-publishing tool on the official FUN Money web site at www .FUNdamentalYou.com.

Don't forget to ask your readers to contribute their views and experiences. Consider rewarding them some way for their contributions. Maybe a T-shirt that advertises your company. Or a free report not otherwise available.

I've seen compelling, interesting newsletters and blogs that are nothing more than day-by-day "diaries" from their creators. They lead the readers through each day in the week, detailing what the publisher did this week to accomplish her goals.

Your entire newsletter could be nothing more than links to resources the readers may be interested in accessing. Your e-book could then be a complete resource directory and your newsletter the weekly update to the e-book, listing new resources you've found, and removing ones that are no longer useful.

Just set up a simple web site through any web hosting company you prefer (this will only cost you around $10 to $20 per month). Then, post each issue of your newsletter on a single page. Send a link to the page in an e-mail to your subscribers—remembering to include some "Boardroom-style" curiosity-teaser headlines to entice readers to click the link and read this issue.

I've placed a couple of great recommendations for web hosting, autoresponder services, shopping carts, and more, on the official FUN Money web site (www.FUNdamentalYou.com).

I recommend you set your goals for each issue conservatively. It's better to publish a short, concise newsletter once each week, on the same day of the week, than it is to compile a huge rambling publication you can only get out the door every now and then.

Readers like to know when to expect the next issue. Weekly publication, on the same day of the week, will train readers to watch for the next issue.

If you're using a blog for your newsletter, make sure you update it routinely. At least once a week, preferably on the same day. More often is good. In all of your blog postings, encourage readers to respond with their own comments. Their feedback on your blog will make them feel more like they *belong*—and belonging is what Web 2.0 is all about. It will also provide your readers with more reason to revisit your blog often, to see what other people are saying in response to your postings and to the comments readers are posting.

I recommend you set up a blog at www.WordPress.com. This is a free and extremely powerful service that takes all the sweat out of hosting your own blog.

CONTINUE DEVELOPING AND FINDING NEW, PROFITABLE PRODUCTS AND SERVICES TO SELL TO YOUR GROWING LIST OF FANS

Once you've got all the news and information pouring in and you've started bringing in readers, your entire business will then rotate around developing and finding new, profitable products and services that you can sell to your readers.

This is the really *fun* part of the process. You are now an information publisher and what you love doing most is the source of your information. Dive in and keep learning—and pass what you learn and discover along to your readers. Once you've set everything up, the process really is that simple.

I know I'm hammering this point home repeatedly, but everything you gather for your e-book, newsletter, and blog is also grist for turning out new information products. You can even compile past newsletter articles and blog postings into new e-books and information products that you later sell. These can be sold to new subscribers or given away as bonuses to entice them to subscribe. These can also become new free e-books that you can test on the front end of your funnel to see if they attract even more readers to sign up for your newsletter or start reading your blog.

As I said in the beginning, it all boils down to three steps:

1. Publish an e-book.
2. Publish an e-zine or blog.
3. Give them *both* away for free.

I also said there were some microsteps involved in each of the main three steps—and I've detailed them here, so you can easily follow the entire process.

The beauty of information publishing is that it's so easy to create unique original products that will maintain their value—products that also carry a hefty markup and that are easy to deliver automatically, so you only have to set things up once and then you can reap rewards for months or even years down the road.

With an information publishing business set up the way I've shown you, your central focus should always be centered around doing what you always loved doing for fun.

It doesn't matter what form the information you publish takes, the steps I've outlined in this book can make it fast and easy to put products and promotional materials together. It works for e-books and newsletters and blogs, but it also works for audio CDs, DVDs, YouTube videos—whatever you want to create that conveys useful information and generates leads and sales for your business.

Information marketing makes it easy to attract an eager, targeted group of people who want to buy from you. Information publishing provides the products you can sell. And the entire process is a *lot* more fun than almost any other business you could ever establish to support what you love doing most.

Follow the steps. Get going now. Don't procrastinate. Every minute you spend sitting around thinking about getting started is another minute of your life that you'll never get back.

Are you truly happy with the life you now have? Get started now and you can easily wrap information publishing and marketing around anything you love doing most, to start generating money that can more than pay for your fun.

Check with your accountant (I'm most definitely *not* an accountant—that doesn't even *sound* like FUN Money to me), but, in most cases, your information publishing business will also make *all* of your fun activities a tax write-off.

That's the way FUN Money is *supposed* to work.

Fade in. A wide shot of Jenny's apartment.

This time, she's sitting in front of a new computer at a new desk in one corner of her living room. Barbies still ever present, but Jenny's obviously set this one area up to run her FUN Money information publishing business.

Gloria, Tom, and Albert stand in a semicircle around her chair, also looking at the screen.

"Every time I make a sale, I get an e-mail notification," Gloria says. "It's fascinating. As soon as I put together that book and announced it on PRWeb, people started downloading it and signing up for my newsletter. Every time I send out my newsletter, sales start coming in."

A chime rings out from the computer. "Bling."

"That's another sale," Gloria says, clapping her hands. Her friends all look at each other and nod approvingly. "It happens all day, every day. Even while I'm sleeping."

"I'm just amazed you set this all up so quickly," Albert says. "Considering the fact that you really don't understand computers and technology all that well."

"I thought for sure I'd be bugging you at all hours of the day and night, trying to figure it out," Jenny says. "But, really, it's so easy I surprised even myself."

The computer rings out with another "Bling." All four friends applaud and high-five.

"This is just—so cool," Tom says. "I can't *wait* to get started. I can't believe you're making any money at all working with people who love dolls—but the proof is in the pudding. I started believing it's really possible the day you turned in your resignation."

"Me, too," says Albert. "I'm going to help Tom set up his 'Seduce Women the *Smart* Way' information business—then he's going to help me get started on my 'Ask-a-Geek' business. I can't wait until we're all working on our own, once and for all."

Jenny turns and smiles at her friends. "Now I can afford to spend *all* my time with Barbie, whenever I want. And there's no boss looking over my shoulder to spoil my fun."

"I can't wait to figure out what I'm going to do," Gloria says. "But I know it'll involve Corvettes."

"We'll help you," Jenny says. "I want us to all get information businesses rolling. Then we can get together whenever we want and swap ideas. We'll form our own little mastermind, dedicated to keeping all of our fun profitable."

Jenny stands up and high-fives all three of her friends. The computer goes "bling" again, signaling another sale.

All four laugh uproariously and high-five one more time.

Fade out.

FUN MONEY PROFILE

C. J. Bronstrup

Atlas Information Services, Inc.
www.BigMoneyWebs.com

Previous jobs held: At age 15, I had my first job as a landscaper (a nice word for the guy who cuts the grass and pulls the weeds) at a local park. It was hard work, and I wasn't interested in it at all, but it was the only thing in town within walking distance.

During college, I interned with the county prosecutor's office, and eventually, I was hired as their chief investigator (nice title but, as I was the *only* investigator, it was a given I'd call myself "chief"). This was when I moved to North Carolina, to become a full-time Internet marketer. So you see, I've always had *fun* in my jobs.

Least favorite thing about working for someone else: The people I worked with in the prosecutor's office were fantastic, and the job was always interesting but not really fulfilling. You had to take the cases that came in. The major felonies, murder, robbery, and such were always demanding, but we had fun nailing the SOBs. The downside was the child molestation and rape cases. Even after putting away the "perp" (if the case could be proved, which was often impossible as a young child makes a terrible witness), knowing that the victims would have emotional consequences to deal with for the rest of their lives was disheartening.

Favorite thing about working for someone else: During this time, I obtained my Private Investigator's license and soon was making more money working for the attorneys coming in and out of the office than the "job" paid. Of course, when I started my agency, my first call was back to the prosecutor's office, knowing they'd just lost their "chief investigator." That was a nice first client to have on retainer.

Sitting all night in a car drinking cold coffee and eating warm sandwiches lost its appeal quickly. I called on my old college professors (I was a criminal justice major before attending the University of Akron Law School, until they asked me to leave, but I digress.) I told each professor I wanted his best student to work for me (*every* C. J. major wants to be a PI—or at least they *think* they do). I sent those students into the field and decided that a lot of this information must be available online somewhere. This was before the "Internet" as we know it, and you had to dial each computer bulletin board separately. But there were a few selling public records searches. In fact, one of these companies would give you a computer when you signed up with them and, back then, a computer cost about $5000. Their sign up fee was only $2000 (these guys knew the lifetime value of their customers).

After about a year, the business flourished, and I found out about a local chapter of PIs and went to their meetings. These hard-boiled, seasoned pros knew *nothing* about computers. If they wanted to run a license plate, they had to call their buddy, the cop, when he was off duty, wait for him to go on duty to run it, then wait for him to call them back when he was off duty. Of course, the cop felt that was worth a steak dinner or a bottle of booze.

When I told them I could do the same thing for $25 for one plate or 3 plates for $50—and they could call my office and get the plates run in 5 minutes—they thought for sure I had some poor sap at the DMV on the take. Of course, I did nothing to dissuade that rumor (Truth be known, I started it.), as I didn't want them to know my cost was 50 cents per plate.

When I moved to Florida, I started an information brokerage (the wholesaler of records—think of it as "dirty little secrets for sale"). I sold that company for a tidy sum, and it's still one of the largest firms in the state today.

The last job I had was amusing. I was working in the IT department of a large hospital. They hired a new IT manager who knew a whole lot less than I did. I figured we both should move on, for the company's sake. I set about automating every process, to the point that, within six weeks, neither of us had anything to do. It didn't take long for management to figure this out and we both got our walking papers.

Single pivotal moment or thing that helped make the switch to pursuing a FUN Money lifestyle: When I was working at the park as a kid, my friend's family owned a greenhouse company that sold bedding plants to retail outlets. One day, I overheard the park manager talking to my supervisor about purchasing plants. I piped up that I could get them wholesale. I found out who they were going to buy from, then simply called that company and said I was supposed to approve the purchase order for the manager. They faxed me a copy with prices.

I cut the price about 20 percent and still made a tidy profit. I promptly quit the "landscaper" job and started selling plants to parks, office buildings, restaurants, apartment complexes, and landscape firms.

During college, I attended two different universities at the same time, since University of Akron and Kent State University were within 15 miles of my home and, when I couldn't get the class I wanted at one, I could usually get it at the other. It was no problem combining the credits later. I quickly discovered that the bookstores bought and sold used course books. By simply scanning the course offerings of both schools each semester, I'd locate courses that were dropped by one, but still being offered at the other. I'd then go to the campus that dropped the course and buy the used books for peanuts (They wouldn't discount the new books, as they could return them for full credit.) Before offering the books I'd bought to the other school bookstore, I'd run ads in the campus newspaper offering the book for sale, as I could get twice as much from a student buying the book as the bookstore paid. Then, when I felt I'd tapped out the market, I'd sell the remainder to the bookstore.

I was totally bitten by the business bug by then.

Emotional reactions when making the decision to quit the day job: I started out on my own, full-time, before I had a family or any real responsibility, so I didn't have the fear of failure based on security. However, I did often run into professionals not taking me seriously because of my young age. Sadly, this has not been a problem for the last 25 years.

Reaction of your friends, family, and loved ones to your decision: My father had been a schoolteacher before retiring as a superintendent. While he always thought the "25 years and retire with one employer" philosophy was the safest route, his father had been an entrepreneur, so he understood it and, while not being supportive, he never discouraged me. When he retired, he was hired back at the school system, to run the insurance consortium he'd put together there—at a larger salary than he originally earned. Then the bug bit him.

He went on to purchase a manufacturing company that makes effects for professional magicians, went to law school, obtained his degree and opened a law practice, and became quite successful on eBay. So, the lesson here is it's never too late to catch the entrepreneur bug.

Time required to attain the FUN Money lifestyle: The first few years were a struggle but, once I got hold of the idea that marketing was the most important aspect of any business and that everything else can be hired out, the success flowed quickly. Success for me is all about options. Money gives you the option to have a business that runs you (in which case, you just bought yourself a job), or that you run. When you decide that your business works for you—not the other way around—*fun* becomes a very high priority.

What you do now: Today, I have a home office, just as I always have, and I also share an office in town with a very successful real estate guru. We do a lot of joint ventures together, and this arrangement simplifies things but, more importantly, we can inspire and encourage each other. It's hard to have *fun* all by yourself. If you don't need employees, I do encourage you to try an arrangement where you share an office with another like-minded entrepreneur, even if you don't do any joint ventures together. Just being around someone who understands your goals makes work a lot more enjoyable.

Your life today: I get up at 5:00 AM every day—not because I *have* to, but because I *want* to. I can't wait to get my day started. I study, have breakfast, work out (sometimes), and get my son off to school. Then, I either go to the office or work from home—my choice. I work on the projects that I want to work on and turn down those that would bore me. I also have an income projection rule I use in deciding which projects I'll accept and who I'll have to work with. If the client trying to engage me seems too serious or unsure of themselves and their own abilities, I'll pass. I *only* work with positive thinkers that I think will be fun to work with.

These are the options that money allows. And, when you start to have fun at work, you'll find your productivity skyrockets, making you even more successful.

Advice for other FUN Money seekers: Find a mentor, a coach, or at least one like-minded individual to work with (Read Napoleon Hill's chapter on mastermind groups, in his book *Think and Grow Rich*, if you need help on how to do this.) Then, make a commitment to *fun* and only do what makes your business fun. In the world of successful entrepreneurs, there is no "should," only "do."

Wrap-Up

- Just recycle what you've done to increase your profits.
- It's always easier to sell more to an existing customer than it is to find a new customer—give them more and each sale becomes easier—and the amount the customer spends, on average, increases.
- Anything you've created can be repurposed into other products:
  - Even your sales letters and marketing materials can be repurposed to sell additional similar products and services.
  - Read your e-book into a digital audio recording and you have a CD.
  - Record a video of a PowerPoint presentation, while you read your e-book, and you have a DVD.
  - There are 216 different ways to repurpose everything you create.
- Your newsletter or blog continues the conversation and keeps selling readers more and more:

— Every new information product you create can also help generate additional newsletter articles.

— People involved in the affiliate products you sell make great interview subjects—and newsletter articles.

— Don't forget to ask your prospects, customers, and readers to contribute—more *free* content.

- Publish your newsletter as straight e-mail text or post it on a web site and send e-mails with compelling headlines and a link to your online newsletter—or to your blog.

- It's better to publish a short, concise newsletter once a week than to get bogged down trying to publish too much and give up or miss your deadlines:

— Consider a blog or newsletter "diary" of your activities.

— Consider a blog or newsletter with nothing but interesting links to other resources of interest to people within your chosen niche or subniche.

EPILOGUE

Creativity is inventing, experimenting, growing, taking risks, breaking rules, making mistakes, and having fun.

—Mary Lou Cook

I know—it's a lot of information covering just three simple steps. But, each step holds so many options, I'd actually need another 1,000 pages to put down everything you can do to launch and build your new information business in detail.

I hope I've provided at least a solid introduction to some new concepts. Possibly some great first steps, capable of leading you into a brand new life. Enough to get you going and seeing results, but not so much that you get bogged down with too many details and choices.

I'll admit some of the paths I've outlined here wander a bit. I did that on purpose. It's impossible to start a business, even the simple, three-step information business I've outlined for you here, moving first through one part of the process completely, then the next, and so forth. Some parts of the process overlap decidedly and require simultaneous preplanning and execution.

So—I've lead you logically through my system in the same way I go through it each time I set up a new system for my own business and for my clients.

Really—it's all about taking that first step. Having a simple system to follow makes taking that first step easier.

As you establish your information publishing business, you'll discover portions of my process you're more comfortable tackling at different times than I've suggested. You'll create new processes to work into the system and abandon some that I provided.

And you'll be living the FUN Money lifestyle. I sincerely hope you do get started and follow the steps I've detailed here to completion. It's impossible to describe the feeling the FUN Money lifestyle gives you. I sincerely want you to experience it for yourself. I want you to set yourself free and this is one of the surest ways to true freedom that I know.

Visit the FUN Money web site (www.FUNdamentalYou.com) and I'll show you a way you can join me, Lori Steffen, and Jeff Wark, more than a dozen guest faculty and VIP alumni faculty, and hundreds of other like-minded information publishers. We'll mastermind together and provide each other with the kind of support and camaraderie that can take us places we could never go alone.

I look forward to working directly with you soon.

FUN MONEY PROFILE

Lee and Robin Collins

Repeat Profit Systems
www.RepeatProfitSystems.com

Previous jobs held:

Robin: My first job was working on the family farm (yes, I really am from "corn-country, Ohio"). My grandpa and dad worked the farm and cared for the livestock. My sisters and I would be assigned jobs to help out. One of my most memorable jobs was feeding the pigs. One of the pigs' favorite "toys" was our shoes (yes, while we were wearing them . . . and *no*, my mom didn't have a clue). It was years later, before my sister and I confessed this ritual to my mom. She was pretty entertained to finally understand how we would wear out our shoes so quickly—but only at the toes! I won't go into the lecture that followed.

I worked the typical fast food gig for about a year while I was in high school, but then I took the first train out of "corn country"... courtesy of the U.S. Air Force. After 10 years of serving my country (and meeting my wonderful husband), I transitioned to several years of consulting as a systems engineer for multiple global companies.

LEE: Not counting my underground wholesale martial arts supply business that I started when I was 15 ("dissolved" by my parents, who thought I was selling drugs), my first "real" job was at a seafood restaurant. I remember clearly standing in a smelly back room shelling (I think that's what it was called) shrimp *all night long*. Over eight hours of just shelling and deveining shrimp. One after another. Hundreds and thousands of nasty, smelly shrimp. One night of that was enough for me, and I never went back—not even to collect that day's pay.

My next thrilling high school job was at McDonald's. I had the exciting task of running the fryer and grilling the burgers. This wasn't a fun job, either, but it's the first place where I started learning about systems and systematizing your business. When we had the right crew in, the place ran like a well-oiled machine. And it was easy to see when somebody wasn't "part of the team concept." It wasn't a bad gig, but it only lasted about a month. To understand why, you'd have to know the one fatal flaw in the McDonald's system. That fatal flaw is scheduling. There were many times when I left work at 8 PM at night and had written down my schedule, and I knew I had the next day off. Then, I'd get an irate phone call, at 3 PM or 4 PM, screaming and yelling that I wasn't at work—I *am* on the schedule to work! Because of the "fluidity" of the scheduling process, and the fact that I was actually told to call in at least once every four hours every day, to verify if the schedule had been changed, I turned in my coveted brown and yellow uniform.

High school job number three was probably the best high school job I had. I stayed there for over a year and eventually was promised a manager's position, if I chose to stay there over going into the air force. It was at a Winn Dixie Deli. Winn Dixie is a grocery chain, predominantly in the South, that basically pioneered the grocery store delicatessen concept. I loved it and ultimately may have had a hand in their success. Even though I was the youngest person working there, after only a few weeks I was allowed to open and close the deli unsupervised (something that had *never* previously been allowed of a high school employee), and I was even allowed to run the deli myself alone on Sundays.

It was on a Sunday, when I was working alone, that I had the brilliant idea to "make some changes around there." On that fateful day, I first married the systematizing concepts I learned at McDonald's to how I thought we could make the deli work better and more efficiently. I developed a pricing flowchart that made customer service at the meat-cutting section at least 75 percent faster. I put a checklist process in place that made opening and closing easier, with less chance for error. Altogether, I put into place seven new processes that I thought would make the deli run better and more efficiently.

I even started decorating names on cakes in a "calligraphy" style that day that *all* the customers loved! And I experimented with what I believe is some of the first "birthday cake airbrushing," using some coloring that I thinned a bit with water, so it would spray smoother.

I closed up that night in eager anticipation of the kudos I would get the next day when Mr. Wally, the deli manager, came in to open up shop and saw the processes, checklists, and airbrushed cakes! When Mr. Wally came in that Monday, I immediately got a phone call. I was getting ready to leave for school, and I was a bit nervous. "What will he think? Did I screw up? Is he mad? Mom said he sounded 'different.' Oh no!"

I cautiously answered the phone, and Mr. Wally said, "We need to talk." "Uh oh," I thought. "I'm about to lose the job I love. I shouldn't have done what I did. I should have left well enough alone. What business did I have to step on Mr. Wally's toes?"

I meekly said, "Okay, what do we need to talk about?"

It was that day, on that phone call, when I learned that sometimes it's better to ask forgiveness than permission. Mr. Wally *loved* what I'd done! He said he looked around, did some quick "figuring," and he felt that the processes I put in place would increase our deli profits by at least 25 percent! He was surprised and so pleased that a high school kid took initiative when other, more experienced employees who had worked at the deli for three-plus years had never thought of any of this! He was actually going to recommend these changes to corporate in a meeting he had coming up the next week.

Wow! There was one problem, though. And it was one he didn't know how to deal with. As it turns out, the only problem he had was a customer at the counter who wanted a cake decorated in "fancy writing and air brushed, like her sister's was yesterday, by the nice, young man." He wanted to know if it would be too much trouble to stop by on my way to school and take care of that for him!

"Of course, Mr. Wally, no problem at all . . . "

I had the Winn Dixie job through my senior year in high school. Exactly two weeks after graduating high school, I went into the U.S. Air Force, where I was trained to be a Communications Computer Electronics Systems Specialist. I later found out this was known simply as a Technical Controller. We basically handled all short- and long-haul communications on the air force grid. This included green-screen monitors, two-wire circuits, four-wire circuits, packet switching networks and, eventually, local area network and wide area network communications—after Al Gore finished inventing the Internet.

Because of this, my first few years in the air force weren't exactly what you'd call "stellar." It turns out that, unlike Mr. Wally, my superiors in the air force were perfectly happy with how inefficient our operation was and didn't need "no punk kid, still wet behind the ears outta' basic training" telling them how to improve their processes. But, in spite of this, it only took about two years for me to be assigned as the official squadron trainer for my specialty, responsible for *all* training plans and ensuring that everyone was "qualified" to do their jobs. Once again, I started implementing ideas and efficiencies into our training system that led to me being recognized with an achievement medal for "outstanding achievement" in my role as squadron trainer.

Every new base I moved to, I eventually ended up with the same role: trainer. It was something I was very good at. Training people and making the processes flow more efficiently and more smoothly. And it was something that I loved to do. It was in this role that I met my lovely wife, Robin, after being assigned to a short tour at Osan Air Base, in Songtan, South Korea (otherwise known as "the speed bump," in any progression of North

Korea hostility). Together, we made an awesome team right from the beginning, and worked together on many high-level projects while on tour in South Korea. We eventually married after we returned to the States.

After nine and a half years in the air force, it was time for something new. So, I turned in my air force blues for a corporate grey suit. It was there, in the corporate world, that I found *huge* success! It wasn't anything much different than I did in high school for Winn Dixie, or in the air force, but this time I was getting paid a *lot* more money for improving processes, training, and also managing a global team for a major technology corporation.

When I finally decided to turn in my suit for blue jeans and FUN Money, I was managing an elite team of nine specialists, I was responsible for over $20 million in corporate assets, and I had grown our area of the company from managing just one corporate client worth $2 million per year, to managing over 80 clients worth over $300 million in annual revenue. It wasn't entirely easy to walk away from such an amazing six-figure job to "do my own thing." After almost seven years doing the same thing, growing someone else's business, I finally got my head straight and decided to do it for myself. I've never once looked back or regretted that decision!

After all is said and done, I believe I owe about 25 percent of my success to McDonald's for teaching me about "systems," about 25 percent of my success to my stubborn Irish heritage that never allows me to shut my mouth—even when I sometimes "should," and at least 40 percent of my success to Robin, who is always my inspiration for aspiring to and achieving things that I may feel at first are beyond my grasp.

Least favorite thing about working for someone else:

ROBIN: Lots! Let's just go with having to ask permission when I could take time for myself; either an afternoon off or a full vacation. To have to schedule my needs around the demands of a company was a real pain in the you know what.

LEE: This is going to sound a bit harsh and a lot conceited, and it's not meant that way at all—but the least favorite thing at *all* my jobs was working for someone who quickly became much less qualified than me to do the job. I did have some great bosses over the years, and I learned a tremendous amount from them—but my least favorite thing has always been working for people who can't see past their own shortsightedness and who let their egos get in the way of processes that can save time and money.

Favorite thing about working for someone else:

ROBIN: People actually have favorite things about working for someone else? That's just crazy talk! Let's see... the nine-to-five humdrum rat race? Or, what about the incredible social cutthroat scheming from your coworkers? I just loved the political clawing to the top. The constant threat of layoffs or downsizing—that was pretty cool, too. Or—how about those emergency pagers going off at two in the morning? Man, I really miss that stuff!

LEE: My favorite thing about working for someone else was getting to make mistakes with someone else's money. I hope that doesn't make me sound like too much of an ass. Honestly, at most of the jobs I held, things were being done so poorly that hardly anyone even noticed when I made a mistake while trying to improve the processes. I got to experiment and, even if I messed up, I still got paid, and the family still got food on the table to eat. I'm still not very politically correct or good at "office politics," but where I am strong is in my ability to be very, very patient. Over time, I always get what I want because, usually, I simply outlast my opponents. I give credit for that to my experience in the air force and in corporate America.

Single pivotal moment or thing that helped make the switch to pursuing a FUN Money lifestyle:

ROBIN: I know that this will come as a shocker, but it was all Lee's fault. It really is a great story that dates back to 2001.

Picture this ... it was early November 2002, but a balmy 60 degrees. Lee and I were living in Richmond, Virginia, and it was just beautiful. Lee had been "dabbling" with the online business route for about a year at this point. I honestly didn't have much faith that we could actually grow his efforts into anything substantial. Sure—a few dollars here and there, but I never saw it replacing our full-time income.

I was so wrong!

Unbeknownst to me, Lee had tried and failed at, shall I say—a lot of different "systems" his first year, trying to get his dreams of an online business off the ground. He was so disgusted by these products failing to deliver what was promised it nearly drove him nuts. But he also realized that many of these systems and books and products had portions that *did* work. So—what he did was take all of these "gems" from the many different sources he'd discovered and assembled his own system.

So—Lee now had his system and he found a product that he wanted to use, to test out the system. But—he was all out of money. Actually, he was $12,000 in debt, after a year of "education and training"—but we won't get into that here. His brilliant idea was to convince me to let him "borrow" $500 dollars that we'd scrimped and saved to use for our kids' Christmas. Things were pretty tight back then, and $500 was a lot of money. Especially when we'd saved all year so the kids would have a nice Christmas.

Would you believe I handed that money right over to him? Yea—right! But, after three days of constant begging and badgering, I did finally give in. Lee somehow convinced me to let him take a chance and try out his "new system" on these little miniracer remote control cars. You may remember them—that year, you probably received hundreds of e-mails for these little cars. (No spam from us, by the way—that's not our style.)

I finally let him have that money with two caveats—that, if he failed and lost the kids' Christmas money, he would have to tell the children why there were no presents under the tree, and . . . he would have to quit his dreams of an online business forever.

He didn't fail. As a result, of his efforts and that Christmas's investment, we had our first five-figure month. And I've been a believer ever since.

LEE: I showed Robin the money and potential for doing what we love and living life on our own terms. That was it. Make mamma happy and everybody's happy.

Emotional reactions when making the decision to quit the day job:

ROBIN: I really didn't have any aspirations to be an entrepreneur until I *was* an entrepreneur. It never even crossed my mind as an option until Lee "tricked" me into believing. I was taught from an early age that you have value as an adult by holding down a job, paying your bills, and taking care of your family. And, where I grew up, this was only possible by finding a good job and doing everything you could do to keep it.

When Lee introduced me to his vision of working for ourselves, I was a huge skeptic. I had 25+ years of brainwashing to overcome. And it was a very intense transition to allow myself to believe that working for myself was not only "okay," but was the only way to really get ahead.

To be completely honest, I went through a roller coaster of emotions when I first decided to quit my day job. Excitement. Fear. Hope. Fear. Confidence. Doubt. Faith. Hesitation. Control.

Eventually, my positive emotions won out and we finally took the plunge. Honestly, I can never see myself being happy holding down a normal job again. And I give Lee all of the credit. Without him, I never would have considered this lifestyle.

LEE: I believe Robin sums it up nicely. Is that egotistical of me?

Reaction of your friends, family, and loved ones to your decision:

ROBIN: Laughter was probably the biggest. Followed by doubt and lots of "how are you gonna' live doing *that*?" You're going to find out, when you decide to travel down this path that you won't have a whole lot of believers until you actually achieve several successes.

We had our first largely successful month back in 2002, but it's taken until this year for my family to finally believe in us. Now, there's a lot of "we always knew you could do it" and "hey, can you show us how we can make some extra money?"

But, in my family's case, it wasn't easy. For my family to support me, I had to break through all of that previous conditioning. Not an easy task. Eventually, I've gotten through, and now I have my family working with me on several projects.

LEE: Even after replacing *two* six-figure incomes with our home business, we still have friends and family who think we're complete morons. But, they're also asking us for work and instructions.

Time required to attain the FUN Money lifestyle:

ROBIN: It probably took us a year to quit our day jobs, from the time we really committed to the FUN Money lifestyle.

When we first started our business, we both held six-figure jobs and were only working the business part time. When you're building a business part time, it can take a while for it to completely replace your income. Plus, we hadn't really committed to the FUN Money lifestyle at that point. It took us getting our heads in the right place and learning tools and techniques to keep us there—before we could really let go. But once we committed to it, things really started to happen for us.

LEE: Once again, Robin captures it nicely. As she said, we've been in "business" since 2001, but only since mid-2005 did we really commit to making this thing work.

What you do now:

ROBIN: Lee and I were always teachers. When we met in the air force, our first joint task was rewriting training manuals and teaching others. This has always been our niche. So, naturally, we gravitated toward this role in our new FUN Money lifestyles.

It's actually a pretty funny story how we got here. After we'd been successfully repeating Lee's system on several projects, back in 2002-2003, Lee came to me and said that if we were both working the online side, we could easily double the money we were making. To be honest, at the time, I had *no desire* to learn the online side of the system. I convinced Lee to write down the steps and then I would be happy to work it with him. This ploy seemed like a stroke of genius. I really thought Lee would *never* take the time to document the steps. Then, I wouldn't have to do the online part, and it would be all his fault. Brilliant . . . right? Well, he *did* document the steps. My plot was foiled . . . or was it?

I said to Lee, "Wow, honey. This is great stuff. 90+ pages of detailed instructions, with screen shots and everything. I bet that even our kids could follow this. Hey . . . maybe we should share this with others."

And there you have it. The birth of our first version of the *One Page Money Makers* system. We began sharing the system that month. And it was years later before I had to do the online stuff!

LEE: We're known as the "Do It Once, Get Paid Forever" people because we teach people how to leverage the simple systems that we've developed to never have to trade hours for dollars again. For example, with our *One Page Money Makers* system that Robin describes, we've taken about an hour to develop a web site around a hot market, got it online, and still profit from it five plus years later.

By now, we have so many hundreds of these sites we don't even remember many of them because we haven't touched or looked at them for years and they still make us money every single month. *That's* the core example of our "do-it-once, get-paid-forever" philosophy. And that's what we do.

Your life today:

ROBIN: People often ask us what our goal is. Our answer is always the same: To be able to be on vacation all of the time and to choose when to work. This sounds pretty strange to a lot of folks, but it really is what most people strive for, if they're honest with themselves.

Let's face it: What's better than having the freedom to take a day to drive to Niagara Falls without having to ask permission first? Or to take a few hours to work in the garden? How about not ever using an alarm clock? This is how we live.

I'm not saying we don't work. We actually work a lot. But, the difference is that we have fun with what we're doing. We can choose to work on what we want and work when we want—or to just blow the day off and go golfing or mow the grass (I love to mow the grass—must be the farm girl in me!).

LEE: Life now is like a 24/7 vacation. Before you misunderstand, let me explain: A vacation to us is doing what we love, as often as we want. Yes, sometimes we work 10 hours a day, *but* we *love* what we do, so it doesn't feel like work at all! It's not like waking up to an alarm clock, to drive an hour in traffic to a job you hate, to work with people you don't like, or a boss you hate, take lunch when (and if) they say you can, get stuck in traffic coming home, and *hoping* you're not too tired to enjoy some time with the wife/husband/significant other/family.

Can you imagine making money from enjoying your hobby each and every day? It's amazing. And, when we want to take a day off, we don't have to ask anyone's permission. We aren't limited on vacation like many of our friends and family. We

201

honestly do what we want, when we want. We do have some limits, though, because we have two wonderful children at home—but they also enjoy the business alongside us, so it's really a family endeavor that we all enjoy together.

Advice for other FUN Money seekers:

ROBIN: Do something now. I don't care if it's something small or if it fails or if you don't make a dime. Thomas Edison once said when he was trying to uncover the secrets of the incandescent light bulb, "I have not failed. I've just found 10,000 ways that won't work."

Failure is not a bad thing. It's how we learn. Do you want me to share the real secret? Positive thinking and goal setting are great. You should absolutely do these two things, and they absolutely should go hand in hand. After all, what good is it to achieve great things if you're miserable?

But—the real secret to joining the nation of FUN Money lifestylers is to get started doing something right now—don't put it off any longer. The money will eventually start flowing in, but you *must* first take action.

LEE: I agree with Robin that taking *action* is essential. Another important piece of advice is take responsibility for yourself because all the bad or good things that you bring into your life are within your power to control, by controlling your reaction to them—and, thus, you control the consequences of those good or bad things.

I read someplace that "bad emotions cause bad decisions—and bad decisions ruin lives." Taking responsibility gives you the power to control your reaction and the authority to make good decisions that will improve your life with each waking day. Honestly, many of my "worst" days are now better than many of my friends' or family's "best" days. This is summed up by Napoleon Hill, who tells us, "In every adversity, there is the seed of equal or greater benefit." Believing in this gives you a silver lining to every cloud and a way to look past the surface details to the seed of benefit beneath.

AFTERWORD

Dear Reader,

Pat yourself on the back. (But not too proudly. You'll understand why in a second.)

You actually read this book to the end.

This may sound condescending until you realize that 57 percent of all books purchased are not read to completion (University of Dayton).

Here's something even more staggering.

I once stood in front of 700 people asking them if they had read Napoleon Hill's *Think and Grow Rich*.

"Sit down if you haven't read it."

I then asked if they believed that by following Hill's instructions they would become rich beyond their wildest dreams.

No one sat down.

Then here was the kicker ... "

On page 36 of the trade paperback version of *Think and Grow Rich*, Hill commands you to commit his self-confidence formula to memory and recite it aloud once a day. Come on up on the stage if you think you can recite it with me now. Otherwise, sit down."

There weren't any takers.

And this is probably why the vast majority of those in the audience that day are still slugging it away at jobs they hate.

There are a few from that day I still remember who are now living the dream.

It's not so easy to identify them when you see them—they are the ones who don't complain, they don't talk too much, they don't get too happy with themselves for the jobs they've done—they just do.

Roughly 1 in every 200 people I meet has this quality.

Alan's method is an excellent one—perhaps one of the easiest paths to financial freedom. But no matter how you slice it, if you're not one of the 1-in-200, it just doesn't matter.

Statistically, it's unlikely you're one of them.

It is possible, however, to cultivate this quality in oneself.

If you don't have "it," it can be acquired through conscious effort in doing so.

And it starts with simple things.

I challenge you now to create a simple, small, unambitious action plan to start a little project based on Alan's advice. Then, see it through to completion.

Once you do, try again with another project.

And then perhaps another.

But don't lose sight of the project that's in front of you at any point. That's all you should think about at any point in time lest the brain weary of "too many things to do."

Over time this "muscle" will grow.

Once you've built this muscle, come find me—I may have some work for you. But then, by then you may not need any work.

—Mark Joyner

Mark Joyner, best-selling author of *Simple·ology*, is one of the world's leading authorities on Internet marketing, responsible for the creation or first implementation of more systems and techniques for successfully selling online than anyone on earth. Learn more about Mark and his Simplelogy training at www.Simpleology.com.

INDEX